TEENS IN
THERAPY

TEENS IN THERAPY

Making It Their Own

RICHARD BROMFIELD

W. W. Norton & Company
New York • London

Copyright © 2005 by Richard Bromfield

For information about permission to
reproduce selections from this book, write to
Permissions, W. W. Norton & Company, Inc.,
500 Fifth Avenue, New York, NY 10110

Manufacturing by Haddon Craftsmen
Book design by Leeann Graham
Production Manager: Leeann Graham

Library of Congress Cataloging-in-Publication Data

Bromfield, Richard.
    Teens in therapy : making it their own / Richard Bromfield
        p.   cm.
    "A Norton professional book."
    Includes bibliographical references and index.
    ISBN 0-393-70464-5
    1. Adolescent psychotherapy. I. Title.

RJ503.B78 2005
616.89′14′0835—dc22   2005049881

W. W. Norton & Company, Inc., 500 Fifth Avenue, New York, N.Y. 10110
www.wwnorton.com

W. W. Norton & Company Ltd., Castle House, 75/76 Wells St., London
W1T 3QT

                2 3 4 5 6 7 8 9 0

CONTENTS

PREFACE

Consider the goals of psychotherapy with adolescents:

- reduce their pain and suffering;
- lift their depressions and calm their anxieties;
- enable them to deal with life problems, family misfortune, and illness;
- accompany them as they struggle to face and grow past trauma;
- help them live with developmental disabilities, and problems of attention and learning;
- support their best efforts to withstand the angst and perils of adolescence along the path toward a solid identity.

Clinicians often meet with their adolescent patients to focus on an immediate dilemma or disturbance. But both parties hold bigger wishes that their shared work will ultimately lead the patient to a more self-determined, contented, connected, accomplished, and fulfilling life.

In the real world of mental health, however, the treatment teenagers receive often falls short of what these lofty and critical goals suggest and require. There are many reasons for this discrepancy. By nature many adolescents sabotage their own therapies. They refuse to attend sessions or raise such a fuss about going that their parents or guardians give up. Many adolescents who come simply don't engage in their treatments. They bore themselves and their therapists, causing premature terminations that leave both child and therapist feeling an unnerving mix of mutual good-riddance and personal failure. A therapy can plod along with both teen and therapist having little idea of why they are meeting or what they are achieving. The atmosphere can look and feel dull and heavy, full of long silences and laundry lists of therapist questions that go nowhere; or it can appear bright and cheery, marked by happy but avoidant play and talk. In both cases therapists are left with teenagers who are not working at therapy, a truth to which the discouraging facts of their lives attest.

All therapists, new and old, of course, know therapeutic moments when they hit boulders or run out of steam. The soundest therapies are full of difficult phases in which patients regress, get in trouble, make bad choices, and grow worse. Therapists can sometimes mistake these moments of crisis for bad omens rather than seeing them as opportunities for growth. Threatening and pessimistic experiences tend to distract both patient and therapist from the work at hand and can lead to significant interventions that can send therapy in quite the wrong direction. Therapists are vulnerable to abandoning the good work that was transpiring, pushing for change when steadiness is what is clinically called for, ultimately short-changing their adolescent patients. Therapies that don't work, if frequent, pose a risk to the therapist, too, for clinicians who feel less effective are prone to dissatisfaction and burnout. I suspect this dynamic explains much of the depression that research suggests is our occupational hazard.

I wrote this book in hopes of countering these perils and reducing the enormous toll that failed or less than optimally successful therapies can take on both adolescents and their therapists. It is based on one basic premise, a truth that, even in a field as varied and controversial as psychotherapy, almost everyone agrees with: Adolescents, like all people, do not change until they want to. Only after they see and acknowledge their difficulties can they take action to do something about them. Armed with that insight, they can then choose to continue their old and habitual ways or they can work to be and do differently, to be and do better. But therapy is not like repairing a toaster, it is not something we *do* to another person. Rather, sound therapy creates the conditions for teenagers to see themselves more clearly and assume greater responsibility for their lives. And for this to happen, *adolescents need to take ownership of their therapies.*

The substantial backbone of the book consists of clinical case material. Just as they have trained me, my adolescent patients serve as the book's primary teachers. Their experiences are what make the book's lessons vivid and memorable.

There are no academic citations in this book. While clinical theory is necessary, too much of it can distance us from patients and their experience. Theoretical preconceptions can lead therapists to see what they need to see and to not see what is actually there, especially when real world data contradict what their dogma, beliefs, or training have taught them to predict and expect. Any one book can only do so much, and there are many wonderful books and journals for therapists wanting to learn more about a particular theory or clinical orientation.

I'll be the first to admit that *Teens in Therapy* is hardly the only book on adolescent treatment. It distinguishes itself by its dogged devotion to the teenagers' perspectives. While discussing varied aspects of technique, the book aspires to address therapists' foremost mission; which is to engage adolescents in therapy and nurture their sense that they own both the therapy and their lives. Readers may best think of this book as a travel guide to accompany their teenage patients on the journeys of their lives. I hope you find it useful.

NOTE TO READERS

I use the terms *teenagers* and *adolescents* to mean children of about ages 11 through 18, though what I say at times may apply to younger or older children. *Children* usually suggests boys and girls under 10. When a discussion applies to a more specific population, I make it clear, for example, *high school seniors, 16-year-old girls* or *middle-schoolers*.

TEENS IN THERAPY

I

WHOSE THERAPY, WHOSE LIFE?

Fostering the Patient's Ownership of Therapy

I don't know why I'm even here.
   If only I had a dollar for every time I've heard a teen in therapy tell me that—most often using those exact words. I've heard that from adolescents dragged to me by parents, guardians, and as a result of a court order. I've heard it from teens in their first hours, and months, and even years, into therapy. I've heard it from teens just starting to face their despair and from others well into therapies that had already brought clear improvement. I've heard teens still saying it in the final weeks of therapies that had accomplished more than we'd ever hoped for.

   Adolescents' *"I don't knows"* can be read in many ways: *"I don't know why I'm even here"* ("What can you, a therapist, offer me? Or, what can you as the person you are do anything useful for me"?) *"I don't know why I'm even here"* ("I'm not troubled." Or, "I'm not the one who needs your help, you should be treating my sister, parents" [fill in the blank]. Or, "This is a place for crazy or hurting people, not for someone like me.") *"I don't even know why I'm here"* ("Nobody told me why I was coming to a therapist." Or, "Nobody tells me anything." Or, the frequent, "Someone might well have told me why I'm coming, but it's too overwhelming for me to hear and deal with.") We could likewise decipher teens' "*I don't need this* and *I don't need you*," as all being variations on the same theme. In other words, many adolescent patients feel that they haven't chosen therapy freely, knowingly, and willingly.

"*I don't know why I'm even here.*" These are big words that can baffle and frustrate us as therapists. What do they mean and what do our young patients wish to tell us? Taking this question seriously can lead the therapist to the heart of the adolescent's attitude and relationship to a beginning therapy. Understanding the answer can help therapists open their teenage patients to treatment.

MEET ADOLESCENTS WHERE THEY ARE

Adolescents often come to therapy because they've been referred by parents, schools, and other authorities who judge their behavior as bad, difficult, unhealthy, or somehow in need of remedy and change. They often arrive on our doorstep expecting their new therapist to be just another agent of that same authority, a disguised arm of the law who sees his or her mission as reforming them in just the ways their parents, teachers, or probation officers desire. How do therapists convince them otherwise?

Consider Isaac, who was attending his third school in four years. If not for the unusual patience of his teachers, he would not have lasted in those schools as long as he had. When we met, he was two months into the seventh grade at a private school for gifted children. And things were going poorly enough for Isaac's new school to urge his parents to pursue treatment. His behavior had to improve, the headmaster had told Isaac's parents, or he wouldn't be welcome back to school after the New Year.

> *"They're all gay," Isaac said with utter conviction in this initial meeting.*
> *"You mean homosexual?" I asked.*
> *"No," Isaac replied with irritation. "They're all stupid."*
> *Isaac held his extended middle finger up and tightly wound a long pipe cleaner around it.*

Isaac's father had filled me in. His son had received a list of behavioral warnings for whipping empty sodas cans at lower school students, repeatedly violating the dress code, using his cell phone during school hours, browsing unacceptable sites on the library computer, and mocking teachers during class. Though these transgressions were numerous, it was teachers' reports of his lying and defiance when confronted that fueled the headmaster's doubts as to Isaac's future there.

I told Isaac up front that I knew he was having a rough time at school. When he denied that and I brought up the incidents one by one, he glibly remarked on the incompetence and motives of every teacher who had reported him. His social studies teacher didn't like boys. His science teacher was jealous of his (Isaac's) genius. His math teacher didn't like teaching. The other teachers were, respectively, prejudiced, disgruntled, "blind," "retarded," or flawed in some other basic way. Isaac saw nothing amiss in his wholesale dismissal of more than a dozen teachers. He saw nothing to question in his assertion that so many teachers could be wrong and that he could be so right. "I don't know why my parents can't find one good school. They keep putting me in schools full of loser teachers. I don't know why I'm even here," he finally said.

"Loser teachers? You must be kidding. You're the problem and everyone but you knows that. Keep it up and you won't have to put up with the lousy teachers at your school because you'll be looking for a new one." I could have said all that and I would have been correct. But I knew from my experience— I'd blown this one before—that my natural reaction would not have helped Isaac and probably would have set us back, a foolish risk to take at this early juncture.

Rather than giving Isaac my view of reality, I instead entered his own version to meet him where he was.

> *"Would you like some help with those loser teachers?" I asked.*
> *"Yes!" Isaac replied with a nod.*

For all of his noise, Isaac's reaction said that he wanted to get along in his school community. His words and gesture were all the handshake we needed to commit to working together. I'd made clear that it was not his parents' discontents and disapproval that mattered most; it was his own.

WHEN TEENS BELIEVE THEY DON'T NEED US

Sometimes adolescents recognize that they have troubles and yet don't feel they need anyone's help, especially a therapist's. They may believe, or at least say, that they don't need professional counseling or therapy, just as 17-year-old Tamara did: "It gets in the way of everything," she said with sadness. "I don't want to live like this for the rest of my life."

Tamara had spent the first half hour of our first meeting describing her poor grades and underachieving. Her clear language and complex thinking demonstrated precisely what she claimed, that she had the ability to excel as a student. She'd also told me about her social anxiety and documented several examples of how it had dampened her joy and life.

> *"It's nothing against you," Tamara said. "But I really don't want therapy. I think I can handle this better on my own."*
>
> *"But you said that you have been trying to do it yourself since you were 15, and it hasn't helped."*
>
> *"It doesn't matter. I'd rather do it myself even if it takes me forever. My parents want me here but I don't. I don't know why I even bothered to come."*

Teenage patients, like all of us, want to be listened to, especially if what they say is negative, oppositional, or somehow disregards the therapy process. Tamara's *"I don't know"* spoke to her discouragement that anything could ever help. It also spoke to the ambivalence that chased her every moment. As her therapy proceeded, we discovered her profound ambivalence about every aspect of life, including whether she should be in therapy and whether she wanted or deserved to feel better. Eventually, we learned that she was just as confused about growing up itself.

REMEMBER WHOSE LIFE IT IS

Although they may not be able or ready to say it, teenagers generally have some idea as to why they have come or have been brought to therapy. They know about such things as their failing grades, drug and alcohol use, probation, stealing and deceit, depressions, anxieties, parents' divorcing, chronic illness, anorexia, better than anyone. But being aware of one's issues does not equal wanting to do anything about them.

When therapists meet a new patient, they understandably view their role as positive, well-intentioned, and constructive. They know they strive to provide help, guidance, support, and kindness as an agent who acts in the child's best interest. Adolescent patients can see it otherwise. They are prone to see coming to treatment as a pronouncement that they are broken and in need of fixing. Because disruptive or worrisome behaviors are often what precipitate a referral, teens can take their coming to therapy as proof of their being bad people needing reform. Who of us could feel good and nondefensive about that? Who of us could see that (therapeutic) endeavor as something inviting and hopeful? It's little wonder that the teenagers who might need therapy the most are usually the ones who seek it least.

> *"Jerry and Angus cheated off Lou's paper but he covered up his answers." Robbie swallowed hard. "He covered up his paper when I tried to cheat. It's always like that." The burly high school junior squinted. "He would've even given Will the answers."*

Will was a malevolent acquaintance of Lou's, hardly the loyal friend that Robbie was.

> *"And that night Angus smoked everyone up. But later when everyone had left, and it was just me, he said he had to save some for Sunday." Robbie choked on his words as if he'd lost a lifelong pet.*

We were out of time and Robbie had spent his entire first hour talking about the mistreatment he'd received at the hands of peers. Robbie had told of generously sharing his weed no less than his food, cigarettes, CDs, money, and help. He'd also described how he'd lie to protect friends and would readily jump into a fight on their side, noting with sadness that no one returned the favors.

Robbie's parents had requested therapy because of his poor schoolwork, addiction to marijuana, drinking, and shady behaviors. They'd warned me that he'd probably deny all of them. Instead, Robbie had brought them all up on his own, all in the context of his relationships with his so-called friends. I could have asked him what he and I were going to do about his many significant problems. I chose not to.

"Everyone wants you be a better student and boy," I observed. *"But grades and success don't matter to you."* Robbie nodded. *"All you want is a good friend."* His shoulders hunched, his head fell, and he cried.

Over the course of his two-year treatment Robbie gave up drinking and smoking, cut back his use of marijuana, grew more honest, stopped fighting, and became a B- student. Virtually every one of our meetings, however, was built around his discussion of peers and the unhappiness of his social life. Robbie was most proud of the gains he made in starting to wean off old, unsatisfying relationships and finding himself the better friends he craved and deserved.

Therapy is a goal-oriented process. But whose goals lead the way? Is it the therapist's (e.g., stronger self-control, enhanced resilience), parents' (e.g., better grades, less rudeness), teachers' (more cooperation, less distraction), or the child's (e.g., relief from anxiety, more popularity)? While the obvious answer is all of the above, we can assume that it is the teenage patient's aims and motives that matter most. In the end, and as we'll discuss

further in the next chapter, we will probably find that everyone's goals are relevant and part of the solution.

ENGAGE TEENS

Any one who's ever tried to get a mule to budge or a horse to
drink knows something about human nature. We can't make
other people change. Similarly, parents and therapists can drag
a teenager to therapy but they can't make him use it.

> *We'd met for over a month. Gerard sat across from me as he*
> *had for every other session, his knit watch cap pulled down*
> *to his eyebrows, his face motionless, slowly kneading his*
> *hands. I sat quiet. I'd tried everything I knew to engage him.*
> *None had worked.*

Gerard had been found guilty of a series of minor crimes, and
his probation conditions required that he be in treatment. In
his first hour he warned me that he came for no other reason
than that he had been ordered to do so, and that he had no interest in talking or using therapy. He never told me this again,
but his behavior was a constant reminder. We continued that
way for another couple of weeks or so until I finally couldn't
take it any longer.

> *"What are you doing?" Gerard asked me, his first real ques-*
> *tion since we'd begun.*
> *"I'm reading," I replied.*
> *"That's fucked up," Gerard observed.*
> *I read on.*
> *"Therapists aren't supposed to read when they do ther-*
> *apy," Gerard went on. "They're supposed to pay attention."*

"I can't do therapy for the two of us," I replied. "It's hard enough taking care of my end."

"Well, you're getting paid to be with me," Gerard continued with his critique, the beginning of what would be his long road to self-determination and self-control.

For reasons too complex to mention here Gerard got much satisfaction out of foiling my wish to do therapy with him. Only when I retreated, when I gave up demanding that he comply, did he come to life and grab me and therapy by the horns. Like most of us, Gerard wasn't going to change unless he could see himself—his problems, attitudes, behaviors, thinking, and ways of living—more as he was. Only when people realize *what is* in their lives can they make decisions to continue their old ways or choose active paths toward change.

Teenagers do not magically become more studious and co-operative, less defiant and less bullying, lifted from depression and free of anxiety, more mature and better connected. Regardless of how skilled or talented a therapist is, until a teenager owns his or her problems, there will be little, if any, change for the better. Only when adolescents take responsibility for themselves can they grow. Taking that responsibility implies taking ownership of themselves, their behaviors, their current lives, and their futures.

Of course, many children, even older ones, are in many ways "victims" of the circumstances and conditions in which they live. Children do not choose their parents, IQ, temperament, neighborhood, school, and socioeconomic status. My experience, however, has convinced me beyond doubt that not just adolescents, but even young children can take less or can take more responsibility for how they cope with what they have been given in terms of such things as challenges, talents, weaknesses, resources, supports, or injustices. As teenagers come to see their therapies as their own so do they take back not just their sense of responsibility in their lives, but they captain their destinies, too.

But how, we have to ask, can we help our adolescent patients see their therapies as their own, especially when we are just starting together? We show curiosity in their side of the story, patience with their way of telling it, and respect for the good reasons they have for not wanting to be there with us. We listen for what they want from therapy and their lives as well as their reactions to what others want or expect from them and their treatments. We try to keep parents in the background or in the waiting room, symbolically making clear that we are the teenager's person. And we take care to show the small but significant little courtesies that we'd show our adult patients, opening a window when they're hot, readily repeating ourselves when our questions have confused them, trying our best to schedule appointment times that fit their actual needs or merely what they prefer.

Fortunately, most therapists like their patients and are adept at welcoming them. This process of owning one's therapy and life, as we will soon see, grows more complex and challenging for both the adolescent and her therapist.

2

NEITHER VOODOO NOR MAGIC

Using Therapy to Help Teens Achieve Change

Many argue that doing therapy is more art than science. I suspect that therapy is a mix of both, a collaboration that advances in medicine and neurobiology will never make obsolete. Despite what critics may say, therapy is neither voodoo medicine nor an elaborate scam of psychic suggestion. The therapist's powers are not mediated through magic or a spiritual ether. There is much we understand as to why what we do as therapists aids the teenagers we do it with.

The discussion that follows will highlight some of these mechanisms. While I will be examining some general ways that therapists affect their adolescent patients, my list is neither exhaustive nor are its items thoroughly addressed. Consider this chapter as a necessary foundation to what will follow and be elaborated on in the remainder of the book.

LISTEN

No one will argue against the wonderful passion of sexual intimacy. Nor will they question the powers of attraction and affection. And yet, my experience with patients, family, and friends suggest there is no more moving (and loving) experience than feeling deeply understood by another person. And no one craves such understanding more than adolescents.

Twelve-year-old Eli sat in the farthest corner of the room with his back toward me. He used magnetic rods and steel balls to build a beautiful and complex dome. As had become our routine, I would ask a handful of questions and he would ignore them. A couple of times, watching Eli struggle with the magnets, I wanted to walk over and lend a hand. But when I'd tried, the shy and self-conscious boy had pulled himself even more tightly into the corner. He'd done the same when I'd praised him more than he could bear.

Finally, his mother knocked on the door, signaling her return to pick him up. "Dr. Brom-" Eli stammered then gave up and walked out to the waiting room and his mother.

"Eli," I said, gesturing him to hold up a second. "Does anyone know how hard it is for you to be in a room with another person?" A wave of deep feeling swept over Eli's face, with both a big smile and tears. No, he nodded.

Eli had Asperger's syndrome and as a result was rather isolated. School, the soccer field, even his own home—or, I should say, the people who were there—could make him nervous. He was a bright boy who wanted to work on this in therapy, and yet, being with a therapist invoked much of the same social anxiety that dogged him everywhere else, a catch-22, if ever there was.

"He said he had a great session with you," Eli's mother called that night to tell me, "and that you're his best friend."

Eli's parents were thrilled, for they'd hoped, but had never imagined, that their son would ever be able to connect with me and his therapy. Eli's social deficits had blocked him from knowing the ease and grace of friend making that other children are born with. And as though that wasn't bad enough, he felt ostracized by many for appearing aloof, eccentric, unfriendly, or asocial. My simple comment confirmed the painful essence of his existence, acknowledging too, by implication, his lifelong yearning to feel happy and comfortable with others. From that hour on, Eli edged closer and closer, until he eventually sat at the same table with me, face to face, and talked about the hurts and frustrations of being him.

Really being heard and understood—not just being given lip-service, automatic back-talk, or automatic hmm-mmms—can be profoundly reparative, facilitating the child's ability to make contact with and integrate what she genuinely feels and who she really is. *"I understand why you are so worried,"* I might say. *"I get why you couldn't stay in school"* or *"Why you had to cut."* As we'll see in a later chapter, such confirmation does not equal an endorsement of the behavior. A therapist's understanding of why a child felt he had to lie is not the same as encouraging or okaying it, nor in itself does it foster more untruthful behavior. Only with understanding and being heard can teenagers brave the next step of facing why they felt they had to lie and why they couldn't come up with a better alternative.

CONFIRM

Despite formidable learning problems that might have crushed the average person, Martin pushed himself to learn and achieve. His success did not come cheaply, however. He went to school early, left late, and hit the books pretty much every afternoon and evening. Few if any tasks came without sweat. His reading probably would have been measured in words rather than pages per hour; his writing was just as labored. Spelling and math were like foreign languages. And yet, for all the enormous frustration that pervaded his studies, Martin kept at them.

"RB, you got to help me," Martin said. He was scared. "Tomorrow we're going to begin writing essays." Martin rocked his chair fast. "I'm not talking just any old writing, RB. I'm talking essays, real essays, with paragraphs and topic sentences. I'm not going to be able to do it."

"But you always figure out a way to do it, Martin."

"This is different. This is writing a whole essay from start to finish with everything in between. We're talking a whole page!" Martin hung his head. "I don't know why I beat my head like this. I should just give up and realize I can't do school like other kids. I just can't." Martin's eyes welled.

"You've met a lot of challenges before, Martin, but this is new and a big one. You're talking about a formal essay." Martin lifted his head and nodded. "One with all kinds of rules, and long, and with separate paragraphs," I went on.

"Yeah, that's why I'm afraid," Martin said, coming back to life.

"Will this be the giant rock that you finally can't nudge?" I asked.

"It might be," Martin said. "But you think if I give it a chance, I might be able to do it?"

"I don't know, Martin. This is a big one."

"But I'm willing to try and that's half the battle, right?"

"That's true," I said. "And it only leaves you half a battle to fight."

"But a half is plenty, right?" Martin asked.

"Plenty," I agreed.

Martin did fine, but that wasn't the point. Think of how much confirming we want when we face something overwhelming. Hearing "Hey, it's only [a major presentation, a court appearance, day surgery], so what's the big deal, you can do it" would not provide us with much comfort. At first, I'd tried reminding Martin of his constant and past successes. But my attempt to reassure Martin dismissed the reality he was trying to get me to grasp: he, so he believed, had finally reached the one hurdle he would not be able to clear.

The human spirit can bear all sorts of hardship and extremes, especially when its efforts and challenges are noticed. Conversely, there are few things that feel as maddening and unloving as having what we're going through minimized or disregarded. By confirming the hardship or pain of bitter divorces, chronic illness, academic challenges, and the like, therapists can dignify adolescents' best efforts to cope with difficult circumstances, and no price can be put on that type of life support.

HOLD

In the best of worlds, therapists can handle a lot. They can hear their patients' darkest fantasies, stories of true pain and tragedy, suicidal wishes, and inconsolable sadness. They can sit with their patients' most intense impulses, physical, aggressive, sexual, without fear, indulgence, or the need to take distracting or counterproductive action. Likewise, they can bear witness to patients' inner conflicts, taking neither side, while tolerating the ambivalence that can torture adolescents. Therapists strive to create a therapeutic space that can absorb intense affect and insulate teenagers from their overwhelming sexual and aggressive drives. These functions in aggregate are what help to therapeutically hold the teenagers we treat.

> *"I hate her. I'm going to kill her. She's such a fucking bitch, I hope she dies." Polly had come to her hour agitated over a fight she and her mother had just had.*
>
> *Knowing this might go on for some time, I found a more comfortable position in my chair.*
>
> *"I know she's going through my room while I'm here. She always goes through my pocketbook and my book bag. She looks in my underwear drawer. She's such a fucking pervert. I hate her! Oh, I want to just kill her." Polly picked up scissors from my desk. "Can I just use this to go home and stab her to death? If I could just kill her, I'd be so much happier."*
>
> *And so the hour went.*

For 50 minutes I listened with interest and empathy as Polly ranted about her hatred for her mother. "I should just fuck everyone from my mother's office and let her discover us, right on her desk." "I'm just going to become a junkie and show up at my mother's teas without sleeves." And, as you've heard, Polly was ever threatening to murder the woman.

But, Polly, you should know, was hardly the perfect child. She did miserably in school, had peer problems, and was defiant. On the other hand, her mother was cold, especially when it came to Polly. "How can you say that to someone you love?" Polly had once asked her mother in my presence, after she'd called Polly a "bipolar nut job." "But I don't love you," her mother had replied nonchalantly.

> *"She's lucky I have you," Polly eventually told me. "If I didn't have this, I probably would have killed her or myself."*

Polly had reasons to hurt and she was at high risk for lots of destructive behavior. Fortunately, the high school student was willing to use therapy and me as safe depositories for her most intense pain and impulses. After screaming and pounding in my office, she'd leave calmer and more reasonable. She quickly understood that my therapy office could contain her loudest and most violent feelings, and that I had no need to squelch them. Nor did I show any fear that she would actually kill her mother (though I grasped why Polly wanted to). Her weekly meeting with me allowed her to release powerfully toxic feelings that would have eaten at her and led to uncontrollable acts of destruction.

OFFER INSIGHT

There are abundant papers in the psychoanalytic and psychotherapeutic literature that debate the concept of insight with much sophistication and subtlety. My conception of insight is comparatively basic and pragmatic. I see it as any moment in which a teen can see any aspect of herself or others more clearly. By my formulation, good examples of insight include:

- A high school student's realization that he smokes weed, not to be cool or expansive, but mostly to cope with unbearable social anxiety and a lack of inner security.
- A narcissistically vulnerable teenager comes to recognize that her constant rages at others have less to do with outside insult and more to do with her own underlying inability to stand the idea that she could ever say or do things to hurt other people.

- A school phobic girl comes to know that sometimes she skips school less out of fear and more because she just doesn't want to go.
- A learning-disabled middle schooler admits that his failing grades reflect his unwillingness to study more than any inherent inability to do the work.
- An eighth grader realizes it's her arrogant treatment of peers and not others' envy of her beauty that makes her unpopular.

The ease with which I recalled and wrote these down doesn't do justice to the colossal effort, time, and pain my teenage patients spend coming to these realizations. Any instance of adolescents' honest self-observation (perhaps a handy definition of insight) can require that they temporarily lay aside longtime defenses, self-deceits, and rationalizations for the ways they think, feel, and live. The power of insight is that it enables adolescents to realistically see what exists, allowing them to then decide what, if anything, they want to do about it. Do I, an adolescent girl may think, continue to be a sadistic and jealous older sister or would I prefer to deal with my feelings in a different way, maybe even start to nurture a more gratifying relationship with my little sister? Do I want to run away from every challenge that scares me or do I want to start taking steps toward meeting them head on?

PROVIDE A CORRECTIVE EMOTIONAL EXPERIENCE

I am not going to enter the controversy here. My experience suggests that something like this can occur in a relationship that proves to be trusting, trustworthy, and encouraging. Spending time with an adult who does not repeat the parents' neglect, abuse, and mistreatment can allow teenagers to begin seeing themselves as more worthy of love, acceptance, attention, and the like. Though this power can be held by a number of people, such as mentors, Big Sisters and Brothers, or coaches, it also can be a beneficial side effect of the therapeutic relationship. When a teen appears not to be doing anything in therapy and yet values coming, I wonder if some kind of emotional feeding and repairing isn't occurring.

> "I'm sorry," 15-year-old Kimberly said. "I didn't mean I didn't want to come. I like it here." Kimberly pulled her hands through her hair, stressed. "I'm just feeling real crummy, like I'm coming down with the flu or something. I meant I might be better off crawling into bed and resting. But I didn't mean I didn't want to be here. I'd much rather be here than sick. I can't believe my big mouth, listen to me. Why do I talk? I only make things worse." Kimberly went on with this self-whipping until the hour's final minutes.
> "I hope you feel better," I said with a smile as she walked to the door.
> "Now I really deserve to have the flu for being such a jerk."
> "The only thing you deserve right now is a cozy bed and some TLC." She forced a smile and left.

Kimberly's mother was extremely self-absorbed and sensitive to feeling criticized. When Kimberly once expressed a bit of frustration over having to repeatedly wait for a ride home from school, her mother angrily denounced herself as the world's worst and most neglectful parent. While her mother's dramatic words sounded as if she felt remorseful beyond reason, her reaction ironically suggested otherwise. Her anger actually punished Kimberly for suggesting a criticism. *"How dare you suggest that I hurt you,"* seemed to be the odd and underlying message. By loudly proclaiming herself a witch of a mother, she wholly diminished Kimberly's right to ever have a complaint worth taking seriously. "If she really felt so bad," Kimberly ultimately noted with sadness, "don't you think she would have stopped coming late all the time." And so, it was no surprise that Kimberly feared that I would react as her mother did, with rage and dismissal. But seeing that I didn't mind her feelings, and that she didn't have to tiptoe around mine, helped Kimberly to see that it was her mother's problem, not hers.

ENABLE GRIEVING

Life is full of losses. When such losses go without sufficient grieving, they can beleaguer a life and impede any chance of future satisfaction and joy. Hold back your tears and sorrow for a loved one's death and you may obstruct your ability to ever care that deeply about any other person. Grieving, letting go of the actual loss, while holding onto your love, memories, etc., is what enables someone to love a new puppy, a new home, or a new relationship.

Expressions of grief, however, can refer to losses of not just people but less tangible matters. Adolescents who realize that they'll never be that hockey star or Hollywood celebrity face the loss of an ideal and a dream. With its new powers of abstract thinking, the adolescent brain can grasp that this is the way it is going to be for the rest of the person's life (e.g., "I am not going to be six feet tall"; "I am never going to be thin and sexy"; "I am going to have to live with my asthma, dyslexia, or broken home for the rest of my life"). When adolescents are unable or unwilling to grieve over their human conditions and limitations, they risk wasting psychic energy by chasing unrealistic self-images and visions, instead of spending time on more attainable, authentic, and satisfying skills, relationships, and selves.

> *"We watched old movies of us as kids over the weekend." Vic closed his eyes. "I can't believe how cute I was. I ran around and was always laughing. I was so happy."*
>
> *Vic covered his face with his hands.*
>
> *"I wish I could do it again," he said, crying. "I'd give anything to have a second chance."*

Vic was a bright and personable high school sophomore who'd been through a lot, most of it his own doing. Over the course of his therapy, he'd come to take responsibility for much in his life, including his bad attitude and mediocre grades. He'd begun to take charge of his life, but it seemed to him to be way too little way too late. "I've got no future," he said, deciding also that he had never accomplished anything of value. Vic's maturation in treatment had evoked in him that inevitable side effect of every sound therapy, regret. *If only he knew then what he knows now.*

Imagine a young woman who wishes she'd learned to play the trumpet but now feels it is too late. At 25, she thinks about it again, aware that if she'd started at 18, she would have learned to play. Again, at 40, had she taken lessons at 25, and so on. But Vic was ahead of that woman. He grieved over his lost opportunities the first time around, and that allowed him to get his life moving in the direction he wanted.

The ways that therapy can help to change teens are many. Each clinical orientation has its own theories and opinions as to how therapy works its powers. Some say it's the technique, others say it's the therapist's being and character, and others see it as a result of the chemistry of the patient–therapist relationship. In the end what probably matters most is having some sort of firm and reliable context that guides our work and signals when it's drifting across lanes or wholly running amok.

3

WHO WANTS WHAT?

Identifying and Prioritizing Treatment Goals

Why am I even here? Therapists can ask themselves that same question. Week after week, hour after hour, they sit across from teenagers who are in all kinds of shape, messes, and pain. *What can I do to help?* therapists can understandably wonder. *How can I make a difference?* That therapists are increasingly facing tougher cases that involve multiple problems with fewer resources and less time only heightens their dilemma. The challenge for recent graduates and therapists in training is even tougher.

Parents or guardians bring their children to therapy because something is amiss. "He got caught coming to school high"; "She hasn't left her room for two weeks"; "She's cutting her legs"; "He threatened his mother with a fork"; "She's unhappy"; "I don't know what's going on with him!"

Early on therapists carefully watch and listen to gather all the information they can. They use that data to help identify goals that the teenager, his family, and they, as therapist, judge as relevant and important. Therapists will notice goals of treatment flying every which way: the child wants more freedom, the parents want better grades, and the school wants good citizenship.

But whose goals matter and which ones do therapists pursue? Take, for instance, 16-year-old Aaron.

Aaron's parents' goals were: good grades (As and Bs); no drugs or alcohol; no more accidents or speeding tickets; cooperating with curfews and home life.

Aaron's goals were: passing in school; not getting in trouble with drugs or alcohol; not losing his driver's license; getting his parents off his back.

For all their differences, we can't help but see the parallel between Aaron's and his parents' goals, both of which seem unrealistic. Aaron's parents expected him to make honor roll when he'd been getting Fs and Ds and for years had shown little academic motivation. They expected him to quit drugs and alcohol, unlikely given that more than 80% of his high school class were users. They expected his accidents and tickets to end (though they continued to fix his smashed cars, pay insurance surcharges for his bad driving, and hand him back the keys aware that some of the time he drove drunk). And as for their expectation that he would be a "good boy" at home, let's just say there was a whole lot of living and self-reckoning to do before getting there.

As Aaron had told me, he had no problem with As and Bs. He just didn't have the interest or energy to make that happen. What he wanted and was willing to work for was avoiding trouble with his parents, the police, and his school. Aaron sought to learn how to make good decisions before things got out of control. He wished to grow stronger at saying no to his friends and to not driving when intoxicated or stoned. That drugs could permanently harm his brain troubled him and had gotten him thinking, though he felt light years from sobriety. In some ways, Aaron's goals appeared more fitting and doable as starting points than did his parents' goals.

There were other goals held out for Aaron. School staff expected him to arrive on time, treat the teachers with respect, pass in his homework, and be medicated (they believed that ADHD accounted for his difficulties). They wanted him to not wear wear his baseball cap in school. A District Court judge had told Aaron he had a goal for him, to not show up in front of him again. And Aaron's probation officer, who perhaps held the wisest view, set the lone goal that Aaron reliably attend his weekly treatment for the next year.

Most therapists would have considered this a hefty enough laundry list of objectives. And yet, in the first two hours no one had mentioned what I took to be foremost: Keep Aaron alive and *wanting* to stay alive. Three weeks earlier Aaron had tried to kill himself.

CONCEPTUALIZE THERAPEUTIC GOALS

A therapeutic goal can take many forms. The most obvious are the goals we're trained to write for insurance companies and utilization reviews, by translating *DSM-IV* symptoms into measurable indicators. So, we target goals like increased attendance at school, fewer aggressive outbursts, less frequent self-destructive gestures, a reduced number of panics. Often, therapists think broadly, wanting to lessen depression and anxiety, improve self-confidence, or, in richer and less limited terms, to help their patients grow more comfortable in their own skins, more attached to their parents, and better able to bear the slings and arrows of daily life. We think in terms of coping with developmental disorders and chronic illness, in terms of mastering trauma and overcoming learning problems. Therapists can rightly see ourselves as balancers, helping an overly shy child venture out and a wild girl to mellow. Therapists routinely work on multiple levels; for example, working on a fear of failure that interferes with a child's functioning at home, school, and on the basketball court.

Time frames can loom large and tricky when therapists think about therapeutic goals. Traditionally, short-term goals are concrete and behavioral, while long-term goals deal with such factors as personality, character, and identity. But, good long-term therapy involves no less clarity and no fewer goals than its briefer brethren. The difference lies more in the types of goals, how they're implemented, and at what pace. A short-term therapy might target a teenager's lack of assertiveness in the classroom, whereas a longer and more ambitious treatment might address the child's assertiveness in all of its manifestations, at school and home and with friends. These goals would all be in the context of her growing up, developing an authentic self, and growing stronger in the face of teenage perils.

Longer term therapies are guided by a hierarchy of goals that ebb in and out of every session. In a single hour we might work on a simple phobia, the adolescent's more encompassing tendency to see catastrophe everywhere, and her inclination toward recklessness. Overall, one therapy might hope to reduce suicidal behavior and thinking, diminish self-hatred, lift depression, mollify conscience, and reduce the need to criticize others. In longer therapies, "soft" goals such as trust and attachment are considered both hard requisites for treatment to forge ahead as well as way stations integral to an evolving therapy and self. Therapists who do longer term therapy know well that the goals of connectedness and positive regard, while in themselves developmental accomplishments, function as critical points of leverage when facing the harder therapeutic times to come.

SET PRIORITIES

In wartime crises of the past, medical units would triage the incoming wounded into three groups: soldiers who'd die even with medical attention, soldiers who'd live even without, and soldiers who'd make it only with medical assistance. The third group received treatment first. Fortunately, therapists don't have to make such decisions. However, therapists face teenagers and families where the problems are many and complex, and the time and resources are limited. How do therapists decide what to work on?

For Aaron, the boy who'd tried to kill himself, survival was paramount. School and the law would wait. Helping Aaron gain mastery over his suicidal impulses was primary. He and I established strategies to sense impending suicidality, ways to contact me in those moments, and ways to distract and soothe himself during moments of unbearable self-hatred and gloom. I did not rebuke his parents for pressing me to do something about his test scores, though their priorities told me something sad about their values and their relationship with their son.

But I would have been mistaken to push the goals of Aaron's parents to the back burner. Aaron got into trouble, he grew sullen quickly, and that was when his wish to die would escalate. And so he and I problem solved ways to do enough schoolwork—not to please his parents or his teachers, and not to earn As and Bs—but to get Cs and Ds, grades high enough to ward off his despair. We carved a similar trail alongside his other behaviors, doing what we could to support his doing good enough (avoiding bad enough) to keep thoughts of suicide at bay. Over time, his and his parents' priorities merged, synchronizing in ways I'd never have predicted.

The goals that parents seek, like improved school performance, come slowly and last. Many teens who come to therapy are conflicted as to whether or not they want to please their parents and teachers, serve authority, comply with rules, follow convention, and work hard. On the other hand, there are many parents whose goals for their children (e.g., relief from depression and anxiety) mesh with their child's and my own.

When therapy is conducted soundly, there is little straightforward about it. What therapists deal with is complicated, tender, and uncertain. If only our task were as easy as rehabilitating an old building. With one case, a therapist might have to attend to suicidal thoughts, generalized anxiety, self-loathing, fear of flying and heights, low back pain, binge drinking, romantic strife, school failure, plus more. Kind of like those amazing street jugglers who keep not just three balls in the air, but also a bowling ball, a curved saber, and a lit torch.

SHARE THE ADOLESCENT'S GOALS

Nothing is more frustrating than having a barber or stylist ignore your request, instead giving you the crew cut or curls or no. 212 champagne brown hair you'd rather be dead than wear. Though the comparison is superficial and weak, we all want our wants perfectly heard and heeded. What is true at the hair salon and restaurant, is even truer in the therapy office.

Teenagers' goals can speak to something basic in their adolescent lives. I saw a boy who, drowning in a sea of troubles, agreed to therapy only if I agreed to take his one goal seriously: gaining the courage to ask out and kiss a girl he'd liked for the past three years. Adolescents have worked hard in therapy with me to motivate themselves to lose weight (and look sexier), acquire muscle mass (and look sexier), grow socially confident (to get more sex), and to get tougher and more assertive. One teen asked that I help her "chill the asshole" in her. I happily did.

The goals that adolescents set for themselves are bound to be more meaningful than the ones their parents hold forth. Parents are more likely to talk about grades and behavior. Teenagers may grunt, shrug, and stammer monosyllables at therapists' best attempts to engage them. But it's also true that when therapists hang in there and pursue the child's interest, or ask what might be lurking beneath the *I don't know*, teens can surprise us. In their own best words they try to capture the angst that tortures them. "I'm such a dork" (in that child's case, that meant, "Help me feel more socially adept and worthy"). "Just kill me" ("I am overwhelmed with life and the demands of adolescence.)" "I don't know, it's like, I don't, like, it's like I got nothing inside, like, I don't know, like [slaps his chest, with tears] its empty in here" ("I am depressed and unable to feel").

Teens in therapy can express their concerns in the frustration of the moment. "My boyfriend hates me"; "I just came from a detention"; "My head's killing me." These sudden headlines can foretell bigger issues to come, in these cases, a low sense of self-worth, an undiagnosed learning disability, and chronic migraines and the stress of being a perfectionist. Sometimes therapists discover adolescents' therapeutic aims by the tone and tenor of their complaints. A middle school student's hectic, scattered, and impassioned description of her awkward social life made clear that she wanted to get better at relationships. One teenager ended her first hour with me by apologizing for her defiant foiling of my questions, which made clear her ultimate wish to better manage her anger with parents.

Parents bring their children and pay for treatment (or their insurance does). They are the child's guardians, and in most

cases, have the child's best interests at heart. And yet, experience teaches us the hard way that replacing the teenager's goals
with those of the parents will get us nowhere very fast. Whatever their goals—whether altruistic or self-centered, big or
small, ephemeral or long-lived—our adolescent patients are the
ones who'll come, sit with us, and endure the discomfort of
therapy. How can we not honor what they wish for a better life?

4

PRECIOUS GOODS

Valuing the Adolescent

As I first described in *Playing for Real* (1990), adolescents are years removed from the show-and-tells in which they'd flaunted missing teeth, pet turtles, miniature palm trees from Florida vacations, and one-finger one-note concertos. But, as any parent or teacher of a teen will attest, these older children do not differ from their kindergarten selves as much as the sheer number of years gone by might suggest.

Teenagers still want to show off their stuff. Go to any middle school talent show and you'll see girls and boys giggling their way through self-conscious and toes-stepping-on-toes lip-syncs. Give them the stage and the spotlight, and many will perform until their throats and legs give out or until the hook pulls them off. It doesn't even seem to matter whether they have any talent. *Look at me, just me!* is what they cry. Their love, if not hunger, for attention has not shrunk at all from the time when they were 5-year-olds waving their hands for the teacher to call them to the front of the classroom. If seventh graders or even high schoolers could have a show-and-tell, we know they would. Sure, the stuff they'd show would probably be some variety of X-rated, scary, and discouraging. But they'd be up there, vying to be heard and seen.

GIVE ATTENTION

When adolescents come to therapy, they also want to be noticed. Tell an angry and off-putting teen that his decal-covered jacket is cool, and watch the calm nod, thanks, and deep appreciation. Invite a cheerleader to tell you about her cheers, and she will come to life. Whatever the nature of their troubles, teens want to find their place in the world, a place where they can be special and count. No one taught me this better than Fiona, a high school freshman whom I treated while I was a psychology intern.

> *As she was prone to do in her first few sessions, Fiona stood at the window dancing in place in a low-key sexy kind of way, singing quietly as she'd do when she wasn't talking.*
> *"They're all bitches?" I asked.*
> *"All of them. They think they're all so cool. But they're all fat, stupid bitches."*

From afar Fiona's words and her behavior might put readers off. But in person she was engaging and sympathetic. Despite her provocative flair she looked and felt more like a little girl trying, against her grain, to be grown up. Her guardian aunt had brought her to therapy when she found her in bed with an unemployed 24-year-old man from their neighborhood. Fiona hadn't understood her aunt's concern.

> *"Like a Virgin . . ." Fiona sang softly while I checked my book to schedule our next meeting. "Let me just finish the song," she*

asked, "it'll only take a minute." When she finished, I applauded and she took a proper bow, something befitting an elementary school recital.

How does a therapist convince a young girl whose slept around to stop? How does a therapist persuade her that she's worth taking care of herself, that her promiscuity will lead to bad places? After more than twenty years of doing therapy, I have few answers to those questions.

Some weeks later Fiona came to her hour wearing an outfit that I recognized from a recent MTV award show. She wore a black leotard, leather vest, fishnet stockings, miniskirt, and black heeled boots. Large hoops hung from her ears and heavy chained necklaces hung around her neck and waist. A red band held her bleached blond hair back.

Despite her dramatic dress her mood was flattened. As always, she looked out the window, but she neither sang nor danced. I could see her hands reach to her face.

"What's the matter, Fiona?" I asked.

After some time, she turned. "It's not fair. It's not fair." Streams of wet mascara ran down her cheeks. "I'm the real fake Madonna. Not them. I am."

As her therapy went on, we learned just how hungry for love Fiona was. Never having gotten what she should have from her parents, she'd turned to the outside world, to adolescent girls and older guys, neither of whom were equipped or wanted to give her the healthy love and attention she sought. Fiona came in tough and invulnerable. My taking seriously the ways she tried to be special touched her deeply, and led to greater closeness and attachment to spur our work.

RECOGNIZE WHAT IS PRECIOUS

It's obvious that I am not talking about material worth here. I refer to the precious that defies blue book value, like the rusty Red Sox key chain that a boy holds dear because his beloved grandfather gave it to him. As one adolescent boy once asked me, "At what age do kids start making nostalgia?" He answered his own question, "At about 5," deciding that the basis of nostalgia making was the losing of something—a person, place, thing, pet, experience—that you'd never have again. As he showed me, growing up even under the best of conditions requires a lot of giving up.

Precious can mean something well done (an award-winning science project or self-portrait). It can include efforts that are substantial and which result in recognition or applause, such as being a member of a state award-winning math club, quarterbacking the football team, playing second flute in the citywide jazz band, or serving as senior class president. But using a criterion of public notice would leave the great majority of us without anything to cherish.

A teenager can hold precious anything that matters to her. It may be a poem that will never see the page of a book or that earned only a C- from her English teacher. It may be a heart that she embroidered on her denim jacket or the cookies she baked for her father's birthday. Precious can be the memory of watching the 2004 Red Sox win the World Series on TV or learning to beat a favorite drum solo on a math book with a pencil. It can be found in display cases, tucked away in jewelry boxes, lost in crowded book bags, or carelessly strewn on a teenager's messy desk. We can also assume that almost anything an adolescent thinks, feels, says, and creates in therapy is precious, too. After all, it is all an extension of themselves.

HELP TEENS CELEBRATE THEMSELVES

Far too many teenagers are incapable of truly taking pride and joy in their accomplishments and themselves. For every adolescent who cannot work or study, there's another who drives herself past midnight, ever accumulating higher grades and more honors that she is unable to relish for more than mere seconds, if at all. Drew was such a teenager.

Thirteen-year-old Drew studied the scene before him. He'd arranged some 40 colored, cardboard blocks to replicate an airport terminal and runway. Every time Drew appeared done, he'd take it apart and reassemble it.

Drew scratched his head. "I'm not crazy about the way the wings of the plane come so close to the walls." He pushed the brick wall down and rebuilt it so as to give the plane a wider berth. He then did the same to accommodate an ambulance that he parked beside the terminal.

Drew was a bright and good child. His mother had brought him to me because he was so unhappy. Despite his brains, looks, and good nature, he hated life. Schoolwork, and his failing quest for perfection, led to nightly tantrums of screaming self-hatred and bloody accusations that his parents didn't care.

"There." Drew turned a block on its end. The small change lent a more pleasing proportion to his intricate model. Again, Drew scrutinized the airport he'd made. "Ahhh." Drew quickly pulled out blocks from here and there, replacing them so that the simulated brick lines ran in the same directions. "That's better." Before he could rest for a second, he rushed

back to flip blocks so that none of their folded seams showed.
Drew fell back in a large overstuffed winged chair and sighed.
"Done."

"We never see him smile," Drew's mother had explained.
"He brings home a beautiful report card but all he sees is the
one A- he got. He's a young boy. He's supposed to be happy,"
she said with tears. "He's way too young to be this miserable."
I knew what she meant for I'd been seeing the same boy. He
neither played nor smiled in his sessions; he only talked soberly
about his shortcomings.

Time was up. Drew, being the good boy he was, started to
take his model apart so that he could put the blocks away.
"Hold on!" I blurted. He stopped. "You can't just tear that
apart. It's gorgeous. Look at that scale, how the terminal
matches the tower, and how the plane and truck fit perfectly
inside." My praise stunned Drew. "Do you have any sense of
what a fine piece of work you've done here." I swept my arm
over the airport.

"Don't you want me to put stuff away?" he asked, his eyes
reddened.

"No way," I replied. "I want it left out so that I can look
at it again later."

It was time to go. Drew walked slowly toward the door as
he let himself survey what he'd made. He walked out the door
then ran back in.

"Did you notice anything about the bricks?" he asked with
a newfound vigor.

"You mean how they all face up?"

"Exactly," Drew confirmed with a glimmer of joy in his face, the first I'd seen in two months. "And I tried to . . ."

My next patient waited. I had to end Drew's thought midway. But I didn't kill his enthusiasm. That hour was the beginning of the road back toward loving himself, as worthy a goal as there is.

BE A SOUL MATE

Young children want it all, all of the time. They want to be 100% certified. They want their parents to examine and touch every scratch, itch, and blemish. They want every moment of hunger and fatigue noted and soothed. *"Watch me take my first steps. Listen to my first words. Delight when I crawl around the corner then celebrate my return."*

Young children want the adults and older children they love to be part of every new adventure and triumph. Somehow when mom oohs and aahs at the rainbow it feels complete. *"Come look, come see it!"* children yell, wanting their parents to be there that very second before the experience is gone. As if emperors and empresses in waiting, they wish to have every minute of their lives documented, validated, and stored away for safe-keeping.

This wish for perpetual self-confirmation does not simply disappear at age 6 or 10 or even 17. The teenagers we know also want us to notice their hurts, their victories, and their despairs. They want their favorite music seen and duly noted. They even want their seemingly most unreasonable perceptions agreed with (which can lead to some frustrating family moments). But who else do these teenagers look to for admiration and confirmation?

Depending on their age and maturity, children may begin to look outside the home toward peers for some of this attention. Looking to peers can involve a healthy drive toward separation from beloved parents or it can signal a premature and indiscriminate need for attention that isn't available at home. Adolescents commonly form intense friendships with peers, and they just have to see or talk to them every instant. They use each other to share the minutiae of their daily existence—the stuff that most parents would lack the patience and stomach for—as well as its roller-coasting frustrations and hurts. For all of their inherent difficulties, these relationships help the teenage to regulate the intense and ever-shifting moods that plague them.

> *"Do you understand it, do you get it?" Pepper asked. "Do you?" She stared at me, demanding an honest reply.*
>
> *"Do you get why I want to die?" Pepper nodded.*
>
> *"Because you feel so ugly, stupid, lonely, and unlovable." I spoke quietly and matter-of-factly, though looking at this pretty, bright, and talented middle-schooler I knew her self-critique was twisted.*
>
> *Pepper shook her head, no. She waited. I knew why.*
>
> *"Because you're stupid, ugly, and unlovable."*
>
> *"At least someone gets it," she said, months from finding any real comfort or self-love.*

The adolescent patient is stuck and torn between two obvious worlds. She looks to the therapist as some kind of transitional amalgam of both the parent she is giving up and the people on the outside who will assume their place. Either way, she wants the therapist to admire her ideas, take her jealousies to heart, grasp her sense of lostness, do everything that will confirm what she feels, thinks, believes, does, and dreams. The adolescent may even want the therapist to cherish the parts of herself that she herself cannot stand, parts that provoke her self-hatred, self-injury, and suicidal thinking. "Appreciate all of me," she says, even through her misbehaviors and worrisome words, "so that maybe someday I can do the same."

5

TRUTH OR CONSEQUENCES

Assessing and Promoting Honesty in Therapy

The first step toward seeing oneself in therapy is to commit to honesty in that endeavor. More than any other trait—such as intelligence, suffering, verbal ability, or psychological insight—I have found the patient's degree of candor, or efforts in that direction, best predict a successful outcome. Because honesty permeates a person's words, actions, and being at such a basic level, therapists can start to appreciate the adolescent's level of honesty from the very first hello through the initial hours.

MAKE AN HONEST START OF IT

"It must have been tough getting up so early to come here"; "It's too beautiful a spring afternoon for therapy"; "What a drag to have to meet me on the first day of the World Series." These are the kinds of comments I make upon meeting a teenage patient. Beyond conveying my understanding that they might not want to be here, such remarks offer a safe and inviting place to get a first and honest reaction. Often teens will politely

reply, "No problem" only to later qualify that they would have
still been sleeping, been able to go the mall with friends, or
maybe, just have been home playing video games in the comfort of their basement (in other words, not here with a therapist). A child's bothering to tell me where they'd really prefer to
be lays the first small stone of a path toward an authentic therapy and relationship.

Obviously, on its surface, hearing the adolescent tell us about
their lives reveals much. Teenagers who volunteer that they
have been cheating, doing drugs, worrying about their sexual-
ity, and so on, surely are presenting with an honest foot forward.
Acknowledging that they have troubles in their lives usually
is an encouraging sign (though, of course, it does not guarantee an earnest therapy to follow). Some teenagers will freely
describe the details of their pornographic web browsing or drug
habits. Some will suggest that things aren't great without saying
how or why. But the majority of the teenagers that therapists
meet will not be so forthcoming. Our search for the truth will
need more than careful listening and watching. For example,
one boy's shrug, when we ask if he ever steals, might appear
dismissive and denying, while another's shrug suggests remorse. Likewise, one girl's repetitive "Fine" to our questions
about school and home can blow us off while a second girl's en-
gages us with its undercurrent of shame. Nonverbal gestures,
facial tension, avoidance of eye contact, or a catch in the voice
are all fair data that therapists can draw on to help figure out
whether an adolescent cares about herself and her life.

Candor does not necessarily equate with confessing mis-
deeds. For many adolescent patients, spoken revelations can relate to personal suffering and life challenges. Some teens can
tell about their anxiety, how it obstructs their school and social
life, the shame and distress it evokes, and the self-defeating

ways they try to manage it. Others will keep their obsessions and compulsions secretive for long into treatment. Does the obviously shy girl talk of her shyness, does the visibly and audibly depressed boy mention his loss of energy or dour life view? Or do they neglect to mention or even deny what anyone, including their therapists, can see? Needless to say, reluctance to say something that is painful or embarrassing, and perhaps hidden from one's awareness, is not deceitful. Being able and willing to broach such subjects, however, often signals a motivation to use therapy and an accompanying hope to find relief or master some challenge.

Although therapists can feel the burden of collecting factual information at a first meeting, leaving room for other kinds of input may be wise. Open ended questions and patient pauses leave space for teenagers to react. Commonly an adolescent's last minute of genuine emotion will betray their previous 49 minutes of seeming bravado or self-deceit, as when a bragging school drop-out shed a lone and real tear over a teacher who'd once believed in him, or when a flicker of self-doubt singes a girl who's normally full of herself. In a majority of cases it is the interpersonal sense of who an adolescent is, the subjective experience of sitting with her, that can illuminate the state of her factual and emotional honesty.

And what about omissions? As with much else in psychology and human existence, they can mean many things. Who of us hasn't "forgotten" to tell something that we'd rather someone didn't know? A veil of omissions can be an adolescent's understandable ploy to protect the opinion that others hold of him or her. Why would a teenager admit she picks her nose or harbors hidden thoughts of greed to a therapist she's just met and who she wants to think well of her? We don't need Freud to persuade us that our patients' omissions can be wholly out of their awareness. Omissions that are big and critical and deliberate, however, can be an ominous sign. Adolescents who purposely neglect to tell us about their upcoming arraignment for assault, having been thrown out of school two months earlier, or using their mother's ATM card to steal drug money, will likely be tougher patients with less optimistic prognoses.

Sixteen-year-old Cara was an attractive and personable girl who took pride in her accomplishments. She seldom drank and it was assumed by her friends that she'd be the designated driver once she got her license.

> *"I'm doing really well in history. I think I might have a B+ after today's quiz." Cara smiled easily.*
> *"And how about your other subjects?"*
> *"Even better. I think I've got the highest average in science, and my English teacher used my essay to show the other kids as an example of how to do it."*

She was an honest girl, she told me also, who practiced safe sex and who felt bad for the immigrant clerks that other kids stole from at the local convenience store. Unfortunately, everything she'd said to me was a lie. We met for a few sessions but she soon enough stood by her conviction that looking at herself and life more directly was not something she wanted. "Honesty is for suckers," she explained, believing that she'd given me some good advice.

PROVE CONFIDENTIAL AND TRUSTWORTHY

What more needs to be said. There are no more essential aspects of the therapeutic relationship. Few patients, whatever their age, will open up to a therapist unless they sense that she can, for lack of better words, know when to keep her mouth shut. The therapist who runs to share everything with the parents or school may find his patients hide from therapy. And self-proclamations of how trustworthy we are or how confidential we can be will offer the child about as much security as the promises of a shady used car salesman. Nor can we demand that the child trust us before she is ready to. The therapist's attitude and behavior over time, including her respect for her teenage patients' mistrust of her, ultimately will prove what her character is really made of.

Confidentiality doesn't mean that a therapist must rigidly take a vow of silence, however. As I've grown older and more clinically experienced, I have learned more flexible ways of preserving the child's privacy and being able to communicate with parents and schools effectively on the child's behalf. While the typical adolescent doesn't want what he says in therapy broadcast to the world or to his family, he often will endorse his therapist's tactful attempts to help his parents understand him better.

INVITE HONESTY

Catching others in their lies is second nature to many of us. But to what good purpose? Trap teenagers in their lies, which is easy to do, and what do therapists accomplish? At best, they make teens suspicious and put them on guard. At worst, therapists alienate and make their patients hate them. Instead of coercing honesty, therapists aim to engineer situations and conversations that foster an adolescent to grow more frank.

Try asking questions in ways that facilitate adolescents telling the truth, without cornering them in impossibly uncomfortable

positions. Asking questions that we already know the answers
to is an insincere trap that can shame a child. If you know that
your young patient is prone not to admit his stealing, ask, "Did
you behave this weekend as you would have liked?" A subdued "not really" allows the teen patient to save face, gives the
therapy all it needs to know, and enables her to express her
wish that she was a more honest human being, one who'd
spent her weekend doing deeds she could proudly speak of to
her therapist. When I work with grossly dishonest teenagers
who cannot own any of their misbehaviors, I'll hand them a pad
of paper and ask that they write down everything they have
stolen, cheated on, and lied about in the past week, adding the
all-important proviso that they not show me the list. Many patients have taken to the task eagerly, and have been amazed
at what they discovered they'd done. My refusal to read their
lists fosters their sense of trust and confidentiality as well as un-
derscores the ultimate truth: being honest with themselves is
what counts.

SEEK THE MEANING OF DISHONESTY

The kind of therapy in this book does not suit the true sociopath or delinquent, meaning one who wholly lacks conscience. Yet, many delinquents have some conscience along
with other redeeming traits. For sure, we'll know moments
when we must confront their double-talking and sidestepping.
More times, though, we'll want to do what we can to enhance
their realizing when and why they duck the truth. Why, we'll
strive to learn, can't they admit the troubles in their lives? Often
we'll find that fear, shame, and other strong emotions prevent
their being truthful.

Any therapist who's worked with a teenager or adult who cuts herself, for example, knows how tenacious and lasting that behavior and urge can be, even when treated with more intensive and residential interventions. Controlling the teen usually doesn't help her to cut less any more than yelling at her might. Such young women frequently keep their cutting and self-injuries to themselves, sometimes for years, sometimes even when in treatment.

Browbeating these patients or repetitively challenging what they say leaves them unsupported and alone. What are the good reasons, we must ask, and be assured, there are such reasons, for our patients not being able to share this horrible hurt and shame? Why do they (have to) say that they are fine when they are in such pain? Why do they say they have been keeping themselves safe even as they have been slicing? Only by withholding our judgment and permitting our wonder can we convince the adolescent child to do the same, maybe enabling her to come out from the dark. This dynamic applies just as well to other instances when teen patients are unable to fess up.

Of course and sadly, therapists sometimes discover that the meaning of an adolescent's dishonesty is pretty much as it appears: to deceive others so as to keep doing what they want. Teenagers who are well on their way to becoming criminals, drug addicts, and the like, may defeat a therapist's finest attempt to promote their coming clean.

EMPATHIZE

I learned this lesson well over 20 years ago. I was then a trainee in graduate school working with an impulse-ridden 12-year-old boy who, that morning, had started a wastebasket fire in his school cafeteria. School and fire officials had generously given me a chance to find out what had happened before deciding how they'd punish Flynn.

"What were you thinking?" I asked Flynn for the third time.

"About what?" Flynn replied again. I'd spent half an hour pressuring him every which way to admit what he'd done. Flynn bounced a beat-up stuffed lion on his feet. I'd found nothing out. I thought of what I'd say to the school principal and fire chief and the trouble that Flynn would soon find himself in. In a moment of desperation, changing my tack, I quietly suggested that the boy who lit that fire might have had his good reasons.

"Yeah," Flynn agreed. "Maybe he worried that the little kids were cold and needed more heat. Maybe he was mad that the teachers didn't care."

"I wonder if that boy wishes he'd done something different."

"I didn't think it would get so big," he said in a whimper, his denial evaporating in a flash. "They just get me so mad."

Frightened by what he'd done and what he imagined would be the consequences, Flynn hadn't been able to admit anything. When he finally felt his experience heard and understood, he was able to lay his gun down. Over the next week, Flynn wrote a letter of apology to his principal, began to explore why his teachers enraged him so, and followed through with the playground cleanup duty that was the heart of his punishment, and one that he judged fair and deserved. To this day, I am awed by empathic understanding's near miraculous power to soften children's and adults' defensive resolve.

NURTURE HONESTY

No less than ourselves, few of our teenage patients are perfectly honest. Therapy is a process that aspires to nurture and shape good things. How do therapists nurture the honesty that's there so it grows strong and more natural?

Therapists try not to punish a child for telling the truth. When he admits that he's done this or that, therapists do not run to tattle to his parents or school or react with horror or angry censure (unless, of course, the crime is of a magnitude that demands it). Therapists do not take the fact that a teenager has opened the door a crack as an invitation to kick it down with critical and probing questions. Instead, they reward the child for taking the risk of being honest by showing interest and patience, and by recognizing the bravery of his act. "You know you didn't have to tell me that," I've said on such occasions.

Therapists can feel as if it's their job to get the child to be more honest, law-abiding, and rule-adhering. That burden can lead us to confuse our role as therapists, causing us to use heavy-handed questions and tactics, making therapy just one more place where the child cannot be herself. The therapist's job is to help the adolescent better see her difficulties with reality, and help her to find better ways of dealing with it. We must take care that a patient's dishonesty outside the office doesn't blind us from seeing her burgeoning honesty within therapy.

We'll know we are making progress when one of our teenage patients self-corrects an earlier lie. I've witnessed lying scoundrels reform themselves in startling ways. One boy brought in a thick notebook tallying every dishonest act he could recall. Another boy wrote letters to people from his past, telling them how he'd deceived or taken advantage of them and asking for their forgiveness. And one adopted teen, a girl who was a shoplifter and compulsive liar, carried in large trash bags full of stuff she'd stolen or permanently borrowed. She ceremoniously sorted it out so she could return years-overdue library books, friends' clothing, and her mother's jewelry. As she discovered, the greatest peril of growing honest is the guilt and remorse we feel for how we lived before.

STAND ON SOLID MORAL GROUND

This perplexes me. I know there are talented therapists who, despite their own dishonest lives, help their patients enormously. I suspect there are extraordinarily honest therapists who are not so adept. And yet, it does seem important that we as therapists offer our adolescent patients an honesty and sincerity to match that which we want from and for them. Do we make up white lies when we run late or err? Do we own the hurtful or unhelpful things we say and do, or do we deny them and throw the blame back on our patients? Do we knowingly break their confidentiality behind their backs then feign surprise when an adolescent confronts us? Does it make a difference? I like to think it does.

Its logic is undeniable. Taking responsibility for one's life requires that one look at it and oneself honestly, and so it goes for therapy, too. My experience has taught me well that a therapy void of honesty or one in which honesty, rather than growing, diminishes, is a failed treatment. If a therapist does nothing more than help his teen patients grow more and more open, with him and themselves, he has traveled far toward finding a successful treatment and a restored life.

6

POLISHING YOUR MIRROR

Facilitating Self-Revelation

Most people like mirrors best when they know they'll see something that is flattering or corresponds to how they wish to look. Some people will go clothes shopping only when they are in the right mood, when they feel strong enough to see their chins and butts in the department store's multifaceted mirror booth. Many people stay away from mirrors just as they sidestep cameras and bathroom scales. That is why we can more easily face the funhouse mirror. We don't take its crazy image of us seriously for we know we're neither a 4-foot by 4-foot by 4-foot cube nor a 38-pound, 6-foot, 3-inch string bean.

If looking in the mirror at a store can be hard, then looking at oneself in therapy is utterly daunting. What can we as therapists do to make this necessary effort easier, less painful, and more therapeutic for the adolescents we treat?

CREATE A SAFE ENVIRONMENT

What does it mean for the therapy office to be a safe place? An office with deadlocks on the doors and wrought iron grilles over the windows? Is it an office that has no scissors or pointed letter openers, or one with padded walls and nothing breakable? By *safe* I refer to a space and context in which adolescents are relatively free to experience themselves without fear that their therapist will criticize, rebuke, embarrass, punish, or take advantage of them for doing so. My work with one 5-year-old boy, the only nonadolescent patient in this book, illustrates this concept better than any I've experienced.

> *Five-year-old Kenny touched the doll then pulled his hand away as if burned. He turned to me with a worried expression.*
> *"It's okay," I said. "It's just a toy."*
> *Kenny smiled nervously as he used both his hands to hold the doll above him by both its arms. He giggled self-consciously, lowered the doll to his lap, and again turned to me.*
> *"This is silly. I feel silly."*

Kenny's parents had brought him to me in a panic. Their pediatrician had referred them to a renowned clinician in Boston who, after meeting Kenny for 20 minutes or so, told them to get used to the idea that their son would at best grow up to be transvestite, but more that he'd be transgendered. Kenny's ever being heterosexual was out of the question the doctor said, adding that his certain homosexuality would be the least of Kenny's and their problems.

> *Kenny picked up the doll and made some quiet singing sounds in a high voice, his version of a girl's. Once more, he put the doll down. "I don't know what to do next," he said. "Can't you tell me?" His lip quivered. "Can't you, please?"*

His parents had told me that Kenny always wanted to be a girl. Once, when he was younger. He'd even pulled at his penis in the bathtub and said that he wished he didn't have one. This was the event that propelled their seeking professional help. And that was all that senior clinician had needed to hear before making his assured and gloomy prediction.

> *"Please!" Kenny leaned against my leg. "Can't you tell me what to play next?"*
>
> *I looked at Kenny. I saw a handsome young boy wearing a skirt that he'd spent his last session making out of copy paper on which he'd drawn pink hearts. On his head he wore a golden princess crown that he'd fashioned from cardboard. Around his neck hung a beaded necklace that he'd made out of Lego pieces, and in his hand he held a magic wand, actually four drawing markers stuck end-to-end. He wore paper pink-hearted bracelets on his wrists, and pretended that he'd put perfume on from a bottle of white crafts paste.*

Kenny had already made much progress since we'd begun meeting. He'd grown more comfortably affectionate with his parents and was showing more boyish behaviors. His parents noticed that he put on the girlie voice mostly when he was frustrated and angry that he was not getting his way at home. He was using it less and throwing fewer and less tumultuous tantrums. He also was growing more openly assertive with peers and siblings. Talk of hating boys, himself, and his body had faded.

> *Kenny started to cry. "I thought it would be fun."*
>
> *"But it isn't?" I asked.*
>
> *"No," he said, sober. "It isn't fun at all." Kenny gently took everything off and put them on the desk with sadness and resignation.*

Though, I have to admit that a divorce and a family move led to Kenny's treatment ending abruptly, the trajectory of his work was defined. The more he allowed himself fantasies of being a girl, the less gratifying it had become. During this same phase, he'd grown more aware of ways in which his wish to be a girl related to his anger at a passive and unavailable father, a sexually abused mother who was very angry at men, and a twin brother with whom he couldn't compete. Being a girl, at least in his head, was a handy, if magical solution to problems that he could not fathom solving as a boy. The safety of therapy had permitted him to increasingly face and try on his secret and shame-ridden fantasies. Though the experiment left him saddened and disillusioned, and initiated a grieving of much in his life, it had helped him to begin growing more accepting of who he was, as a boy who in many ways felt like a girl, as a boy who felt overwhelmed by much in his life and family.

RESPECT WHAT PATIENTS NEED TO SEE

It is not rare that we meet adolescents who hold onto their perceptions of themselves with tight fists. We see the folly of what they perceive but we go along quietly. We know that fast held illusions have their reasons. Why else would they be grasped so rigidly and desperately? Consider Julie, an eighth grader from a well-to-do and apparently intact suburban family.

> *Julie stood at my desk. Using the gift paper and tape that she'd brought with her, she used her therapy hour to wrap Valentine gifts she'd bought for her parents. As she made and wrote gift cards, she read them aloud. Each declared her deep love and affection.*
>
> *"They love me so much!" she crowed.*

It was hard for me to witness that scene. I knew the emotional neglect that had been Julie's life. I also was sure that her parents would not be putting the same thought and effort into her February 14th, in fact, it would turn out, that they wouldn't remember her at all. I wanted to shake Julie and tell her to get over it, to let her parents go for they, it was sure, would never love her as she deserved and yearned for. But I knew better. To admit that neither her mother nor her father loved her would have been too much to bear.

Having finished her parents' gifts, Julie threw an unwrapped candy bar on my desk. "Happy Valentine's Day," she said unceremoniously. "I was going to make you a card but I never got around to it. You know how it is." Sad to say, I felt diminished for a moment, until I saw a second candy bar fall from her coat. "Ooops," she said. "I don't want to lose that. That's for Mrs. Flaherty." Julie casually threw the candy back in her pocket.

Mrs. Flaherty was an older woman who worked in the kitchen at Julie's church. Even though they'd never spent more than a handful of minutes before and after each weekly youth group meeting, they'd been friends for years. Mrs. Flaherty had often brought Julie homemade treats, books that her grandchildren had enjoyed, and hand-me-down clothing from her daughters. "It's a lucky mom who has a daughter like you," she'd once told Julie, and Julie had held onto those words even more tightly than she did her dream of being her parents' favorite. More than being cruel, to have popped that illusion, would have been clinically destructive.

DON'T RUSH TO PROTECT CHILDREN FROM WHAT THEY SEE

When we hear a parent blame herself for her child's autism or mental retardation, we comfortably counter her faulty reasoning. When we hear neglectful or abusive parents blame themselves for a child's woes, we may feel less eager to challenge their thinking. And yet, we may wish to protect them from the unbearable hurt such awareness can bring. The same is true when we work with teenagers like Myles.

Myles was a high school student whom I began to treat after a hospitalization for his attempt to hang himself. When I'd met him he was a school-failing, stealing, drinking, defiant teen on the verge of violence. For the first year of treatment we moved slowly. Feelings and revelations easily overcame him and would quickly lead to regression, rage, and suicidal impulses. The need to walk on eggshells at times especially frustrated his mother and father who felt handcuffed in their parenting. When Myles felt better he'd grow more arrogant and irresponsible. But when his parents came down on him, he'd disintegrate and start talking about his wish to die. They'd understandably back off, and so on and so forth. No parent wants to risk pushing their child to the edge of a bridge. It took a good deal of therapy before Myles could begin to see himself for who he was.

> "And I can be a real asshole," Myles continued, having already that hour argued why I should also think him self-centered, immature, and a coward. "Don't you think?"
> I nodded, agreeing with all that he'd said. "Yeah, you can be."

This hour was not nearly as dramatic as it may sound. Myles was ready for this clarity in self-perception and I saw no good reason to persuade him otherwise. For months I'd heard first-hand about the cruelty he'd show others, especially his family, and the ways in which he'd mercilessly intimidate younger children. Myles had finally grown enough to begin facing him-self. There was no justifiable reason for my preventing him from doing so. Running to save teenagers from their own self-condemnation may feel supportive in the short term, but in the long run what are we telling them?

POKE PATIENTS' PERCEPTIONS

Therapists tend to agree that we show respect for our patients' perceptions even when they clash with our own and others' views. Teenage patients' version of reality, we understand, represents the truth that they know, a truth that is as significant and worthy as it is unverifiable. Yet, even as we strive to honor our teenage pa-tients' ways of seeing themselves, we reserve the (clinical) right and obligation to sometimes test their eyesight.

Belinda was a 12-year-old girl with a history of anxiety and stomach pain, and more recently, a diagnosis of chronic fatigue syndrome, a collection of symptoms for which there is no defini-tive medical test or treatment. Belinda took that diagnosis to heart. She'd walk into my office at a inchworm's pace, shuffling her feet, eyes barely open, appearing in search of steady ground, easing herself shakily into a chair as if finding an oasis after weeks lost in the Sahara. She felt horrid, it was real, and I appreciated that. But she saw herself as much sicker than she was, and that misperception had branded itself into her self-image. When I learned that for months she'd avoided the daily, low intensity aer-obic exercise that her doctor, a national expert on the syndrome, had recommended, I spoke up.

"Belinda, I've seen dying people, people with cancer and people recovering from open heart surgery who walk faster than you."

"Yeah, so what's your point?"

"I've seen 95-year-olds live with more pep," I continued.

"Yeah, well I'm not most people."

My questioning Belinda's sickly self-image eventually led to her acknowledged reluctance to get herself better, and insights to the reasons why. That she began exercising at a local health club was just a bonus to the therapy. Belinda, like most patients I have met, did not resent my plodding toward reality as long as she felt I was being fair, honest, and caring in my assertions.

CONFIRM PATIENTS' PERCEPTIONS

Many children grow up in homes where they are dissuaded, if not punished, from seeing clearly. The child is in so many ways told that they do not see drunk or abusing parents, anger and neglect. In subtler ways, narcissistic families can subtly demand that their children devote themselves to sensing and meeting a parent's needs. Out of fear of parents' rage or losing their love, these children become experts at forsaking what they think and feel. For teenagers to lose touch with themselves and come to mistrust their own reactions to life can be one of the most unsettling and chilling of human experiences. *"Who am I?"* these teens wonder. *"What do I really think and believe? What do I really feel?"*

How does a therapist answer these questions, or more aptly put, how does a therapist help his teenage patients answer their own questions? Mostly, by accompanying adolescents through their experiences and relationships via active listening and empathic responses. It may not matter that I've set the office thermostat to 73 degrees, and that I'm comfortable. My patients say they're chilly. My natural reaction might be to express amazement that they could be cold, wonder aloud whether they're falling ill, and query whether they ate breakfast. But, by asking patients to rethink how they feel, or to point out how their feelings wrongly contrast with my own, I risk repeating the narcissistic relationships they suffer at home. I'd also miss the therapeutic boat. By simply offering a shawl, closing a window, or throwing another log on the fire, I show patients who can't trust their feelings that their sense of being cold is accurate, important, and worth my confirming and tending to it.

Of course, teen patients can ask that we confirm more than what their bodies feel. They will want their therapists to share their mirror, understanding and confirming all of their experiences—how mean the other girls are, how impossible the math homework is, how uncaring the teachers can be, how selfishly her parents live. If therapy goes well, they will want you to own, also, the inevitable moments when you fail them. As these adolescents grow more trusting of their own self-perceptions, they will grow more agile at handling the grit of life. But, for sure, the therapeutic road can be long and painful. Consider, when childhood goes well, how full each day is of parents' confirming and responding to their children. When that goes awry, there's a lot of catching up to do.

POLISH YOUR OWN MIRROR: THERAPIST MISPERCEPTIONS

Being a therapist to teenagers is a noble endeavor and carries great responsibility. If therapists are the guides on the child's journey toward self-discovery and understanding, shouldn't they strive to be as solid, steady, and self-knowing as possible? We can easily imagine the effect that a therapist's need to be right might have on his patients. How about a narcissistic therapist who needs his patients to confirm *his* perceptions? His own vanities, insecurities, blind spots, psychological scars of his past, and strains in his own family can adversely influence a therapist as can pressures from the outside. Therapists are liable to see their patients inaccurately through lenses (mis)colored by the constraints of HMOs, the increasing workloads at their clinics, their weakening private practice, or perhaps, the costs of their alimony and children's college tuition.

We as therapists are compelled to use whatever means we can to guard against our own misperceptions in the office. Talk with trusted colleagues, seek consultation, and, of course, partake in your own treatment. Many therapists have never had their own therapies, and are the first to claim they're too busy or don't have the money. Observe the trends of your work. Note the types of difficulties you most experience and the kinds of teenagers you experience them with. Try pondering to yourself, whether you dislike or fear adolescents, see them as master manipulators, or, conversely, whether you like them too much and wish to be more their buddy than a therapeutic ally. And for therapists who have children, ask whether you use your teenage patients to seek closeness or other things lacking with your son or daughter? Therapists can likely come up with better and more relevant questions to ask and monitor themselves.

7

TREAD GENTLY

Respecting Self-Esteem and Its Vulnerability

A few years back the satirical newspaper, *The Onion*, ran a humorous editorial titled, "I Know What's Best for Everybody," in which the fictional op-ed author gave suggestions for pretty much everything. When a relative of mine was visiting and saw my son laughing at the piece, he asked, "What's so funny about that? Some people do know more." That man—who nearly always has a suggestion how other people can better invest, clean, think, work, and cut a tomato—couldn't understand why others didn't appreciate his input. "I don't get it," he said. "I'm happy when someone can give me good advice." As you might guess, no one ever could.

I'm not criticizing that man. Most of us are the same. While some do better with constructive criticism, none of us enjoys it. We want raves, not critiques. At best we learn, as I have done in my writing, to weather and heed the opinion of others, such as editors. And yet, if our books, casseroles, or haircuts get anything less than four-star reviews, it stings us.

If we as mature adults are so prickly, what does that leave for the adolescents? Have you tried to help a teenager with homework lately? You may recognize this scene from my original, yet-to-be-written play, *Home Life*.

Act I

A New England kitchen. A 14-year-old girl in an oversized plaid flannel shirt sits at the kitchen table. An overflowing book bag rests against the leg of her chair. Books and papers cover the table. Her father sits in the adjacent family room reading the newspaper.

    Girl: I can't do this stupid math.
    Father: Would you like some help?
    Girl: I hate this!

The girl flings her pencil at the wall. Her father closes his newspaper.

    Father: Would you like some help?
    Girl: It won't help.
    Father: Let me take a peek.

The father walks over to the table, sits down, and pulls the book toward him. His daughter jerks the book back toward herself.

    Girl: No, not that one!

The father walks back to his chair.

    Girl: You're not going to help me?

The father returns to the table for what we know will be a yo-yo of an evening. As he turns to try and help her once more, we see the back of his head and scattered bald spots where he's torn out clumps of his own hair. The curtain closes.

If I were the New York's theater critic and was asked to give a one-line synopsis for this play, it would have to be: "*A teenage girl feels stupid and can't stand it.*" If we, as parents or as therapists, could learn one insight to help us cope with adolescents, this might be the one. Just think how often remembering this maxim—or, is it a mantra?—would help us get it right.

> *Teenage* boy *feels* small *and can't stand it.*
> *Teenage* girl *feels* ugly *and can't stand it.*
> *Teenage* girl *feels* selfish *and can't stand it.*
> *Teenage* boy *feels* mean *and can't stand it.*
> *Teenage* girl *feels* hated *and can't stand it.*

We can assume that the adolescents who come to our offices will somehow, some time, some way feel *inadequate, flawed, crazy, beyond our help, too dependent* for their coming, and that they won't be able to stand it.

GO EASY AND BE GENTLE

I first saw Hector when he was a high school sophomore. He was an extraordinary athlete who barely passed his classes. Hector frustrated the adults in his life—his parents, teacher, and coaches. They knew that with a little more effort in school, he'd receive an athletic scholarship to college. But he refused to do the most trivial assignments, and when he would do the work, he'd neglect to turn it in or he'd hand it to the teacher covered with coffee and ketchup stains. An occasional good grade was usually a result of his cheating or plagiarizing from the World Wide Web. "What difference does it make?" he'd ask me. "I"m just a retard anyways."

His home life was terribly strained. Hector and his mother only wished they got along as well as oil and water. He saw her as intrusive and controlling. She saw him as lazy and corrupt. Hector's relationship with his father was better, yet full of tensions. "I'm just a major fuck-up and disappointment to him," Hector said. His father, a man who envied his son's athletic gifts and opportunities, couldn't stand to watch Hector "piss them away."

Hector's referral to me came on a wave of troubling behaviors. His school was threatening expulsion. His parents had found beer cans under his bed, and his mother couldn't stand his inconsiderateness and refusal to follow the rules of the house. His father worried about Hector's depression, as seen in his dispirited nature and casual remarks that he'd be better off dead. Recently, while running in the woods, Hector had come across the decimated body of a man who'd thrown himself in front of a train. That was the final straw in convincing his parents that he needed counseling.

> *"I don't need to be coming," Hector told me once more in what was his fifth or sixth month of weekly therapy. "I really don't, you know."*
>
> *What could I say? Over more than twenty hours I'd heard him say it fifty different ways. In the third or fourth hour I'd played at being a reality therapist, pointing out all the reasons he needed my help. My tough talk got him to squirm, tear up, and skip the next three hours. "And I'd thought you were a nice guy," he confessed upon his return, speaking his most candid words yet.*

In spite of his manly athletic build, Hector resembled a frightened little boy. His eyes would open big in terror, his skin would blanch, and he would appear to be a blink away from hysterical sobbing. Over many months, a best friend's sister and family members died of cancer, two acquaintances committed suicide, and a car accident killed a friend, but the tears never came, and Hector jumped away from those tragedies as quickly as he could.

"You've witnessed so much horror," I said after one of the deaths. I knew that his means of escape—drinking, smoking weed, and sex—were on the rise. Hector's legs revved like butterflies on speed. He looked out the window.

"It's okay to cry," I said, certain that the translucent floodgates would crack and give way to the sobbing and relief long overdue.

And yet Hector didn't shed anything. I later learned that he had tricks—pinching his fingers, fantasizing about sex, rolling joints in his head—to distract himself from the sadness and possibly breaking down.

"It hurts so, so much," I went on. The tension was a volcanic boil needing to be lanced. I held out a box of tissues.

Hector checked his watch. "Gotta go, thanks," he said and bolted. He canceled the following hour and came late to the next. He didn't say anything about death, loss, or my comments and instead talked of two weeks of debaucheries and his deteriorating schoolwork.

I'd like to report that we never repeated this, but we did many times. However gently I tried to go, I went too fast, too hard, and too deep. If we were attaining a progress that ran underground, all I saw were his retreats, absences, and self-anesthesia. Only after much work, and my learning to go more gently, did we make our first visible breakthrough. Hector had come to his hour distraught. An all-state athlete, he'd been playing poorly and had just walked off the field.

> *Hector sat motionless as if bound by an invisible straitjacket. I could feel his rage. He appeared ready to explode or fall into a catatonic immobility. It was more than 40 minutes into his session and Hector had been unable to find any release. No words to speak, no actions to take. I took a risk.*
>
> *"I'm at a loss, Hector," I spoke matter-of-fact to counter the heaviness. "It's like something's stuck in you and when I speak, I only push it in farther."*
>
> *A few tears that could be counted rolled along his nose.*
>
> *"I'm stuck all right," he sighed. "Fucking stuck."*

Hector's therapy was hard and slow. Its gains were snail-like and hard won. Hector's pain, like a massive wound or burn, irritable and raw, needed treatment and yet, the tenderest touch hurt too much. But Hector's sensitivity was hardly rare. It is common to life and requires that we as therapists hone a soft and deft touch, so that we can dress the human wounds that need attention.

ALLEVIATE THE TORTURE OF
THE SELF-CENTERED

Therapists frequently encounter teenagers with self-esteems as thick and sturdy as day-old phyllo dough. These narcissistically damaged children appear to have one thing on their minds: *themselves*. But as the Swiss analyst Alice Miller eloquently taught us in her *Drama of the Gifted Child*, we must beware of judging their apparent self-absorption too readily. She has given clear and fair warning that we cannot possibly understand these boys and girls (and how they treat others) without studying the ways in which they themselves were or continue to be treated.

> *"Even the freshman on the team give me lip. Shit, when I was in the ninth grade I showed respect for the upperclassman. If one of the captains spoke to me, I listened like she was my boss or something."*
>
> *Esther had come right from soccer practice wearing her uniform. I hadn't squeezed one word into her lengthy tirade about the many girls who, she said, perpetually mistreated her. Jamie, who didn't invite her to her party; Carrie, who thinks she's so cool in her Abercrombie clothes. Then there were the secrets and gossips that she's shut out of. "Fuck them all," she said. "I hope they all get AIDS and die, especially Stef, that greasy slut. I can't believe Mrs. Bernardi thinks she's smart. Fat ass moron." Esther's foot knocked over the soda can she'd put on the floor. Soda fizzed out. "Don't worry, it can be cleaned. We had that happen at my house." Esther made no move to pick up the can or to clean it up. I got up and did both.*
>
> *"Can I go on now?" she asked when I sat down, as if I'd gone off to make myself a nice lunch.*
>
> *"Please," I said.*
>
> *"And I'm probably not even going to be captain next year. I'll be the first senior in the history of the school not to be captain." Esther felt the nail on her little finger. "They should shoot that lady."*
>
> *"Who?" I asked.*
>
> *"The lady who did my nails. They pay her too much."*

Esther looked at the clock. "How much time is left?"

"About seven minutes," I replied, struck that Esther still didn't seem to know what time her hour ended or how long it lasted. She fell back in her chair, done, out of steam, no curiosity as to my reaction, business as usual.

It was nearing the end and time for my weekly gamble. I spoke. "Esther, you wish others would treat you better."

"I didn't say that," she shot back. "I don't have problems getting along with people. Fuck, my life isn't bad enough without my therapist dumping on me."

Esther huffed as she put on her jacket and shoulder bag. "That was a big help. I feel much better. Thanks a ton." She stormed off.

A couple of pages in a book can't do justice to a therapy as rich and complex as Esther's, but I'll try. Just months after Esther was adopted her mother had gotten pregnant, something she'd given up on. To make a very long and sad story short, Esther quickly became the ugly duckling of the family. Her mother, a bright and accomplished professional, much preferred the temperament and quickness of her biological baby, a boy. Esther's needs fell by the wayside. With no apparent remorse or regret, her mother would tell me how as a toddler Esther preferred other children's mothers and how it was just as well with her. Esther would complain how much better loved her brother was. Anyone spending mere minutes with her mother knew that Esther spoke the truth. When speaking about her son, Esther's mother's eyes shone and her pride glowed as she transformed his mishaps to adventures and his misbehaviors to developmental phases.

Everything about Esther, on the other hand, got the Midas touch in reverse. According to her mother, Esther was always the selfish, slow, unhelpful, boring child. "I know I should feel bad," her mother said, "but you know me, I just call 'em as I see 'em."

It was 4:30 and already dark on a cold mid-December day. Esther slung back in her chair. Her eyelids kept falling. "I'm so tired," she said. "I thought I was going to fall asleep in my last class today." I smiled and she smiled back. She yawned big and with a little squeak. "I sound like my dog." We laughed.

Esther took her agenda book out and studied it aloud. "I have gym first period and a study second. I think I'm going to sleep late and go in for science." She put the book away, then leaned into the chair. "Sleep. My kingdom for sleep."

"Did you stay up late last night?"

"Stay up late?" Esther yelled, suddenly awake. "Why does everyone think it's my fault? Can't someone just be tired? I guess I'm just a major fuck up. A royal fuck up!"

Esther left with a scowl and no good-bye.

Over many months I'd occasionally meet with Esther and her mother in the hope of repairing their relationship. Each time I was socked by the unfamiliar Esther I'd see—conciliatory, without sarcasm, working hard to get her mother's attention— and the total lack of empathy that her mother gave in return. In one of those meetings, Esther poured her heart out, taking the blame for their disharmony. "Is there such a thing as chronic PMS?" her mother replied as she checked her cell phone messages. Once Esther brought her mother a bunch of small and pretty flowers to their meeting. Her mother took them without a word while launching into an assassination of the trim Esther's "piggish" eating habits. After they departed, I found Esther's bouquet lying on the floor under her mother's chair.

Esther had good reason to feel down and to expect the world to trample her. Having never received the validating and empathy she needed, she was unable to give the same in kind to others. While her inability to take other people's perspectives, her rabid feelings of jealousy and envy, and her intensely overgrown need for love were all under understandable, they nonetheless obstructed friendships with peers, especially other girls. Most of all, the curse of Esther's self-centeredness was not the lack of mutuality she felt with peers, it was living under the gargantuan magnifying glass of self-critique along with the ever-present torment of feeling herself to be the cause of everything bad.

Coming for therapy itself can threaten a teenager's self-esteem. For a child like Esther, the threat is colossal, the vulnerability exquisite, and the sense of being slighted, rejected, insulted, and exploited, unrelenting. Whereas narcissistic injuries are an incidental in most teenagers' lives and therapies, they lay at the core of Esther's, constituting the very essence of her therapeutic work with me. Over time and sessions, her sensitivity lessened and she grew able to discuss and resolve the hurt, ridicule, or blame she felt at my hands and at the hands of others. Each instance of an unintentional hurt and its repair helped to convince Esther that she wasn't the cause of every interpersonal conflict and that relationships could continually be repaired and renewed. As her self-hatred receded, her friendships improved. It wasn't until years later, when her brother rebelled, that Esther's mother opened her arms to her daughter. Fortunately, Esther had grown enough to accept them. Such growth takes time and patience, however. And that's a lot to ask of both the teenager and her therapist.

In many cases, if not in a majority of cases, issues of esteem are an essential feature of the adolescent in therapy. How the therapist handles these susceptibilities will have everything to do with the treatment's efficacy. Even in cases where narcissistic frailty is not at the core, it is frequently woven into the patient's psychic fabric and armor. Therapists who learn to better read their teen patient's level of esteem will find that their therapeutic aim gains acuity and potency. After all, nothing scares off teen patients like comments or observations that overwhelmingly disregard or injure their self-esteem. Conversely, therapists who heed the impact of their words and actions on teens' self-esteem will more likely have patients who stick with treatment, feel valued by the therapist, and work at getting better.

8

LIGHTS, CAMERA, ACTION!

Spotlighting Conflict

As a therapist, I think of conflict in simple terms—anytime anything comes up against something else. Some of our patients' conflicts—their battling with the law, the police, or other kids—are as obvious and neat as the civil wars that the evening news reports on. Fighting with parents and house rules and wrestling with the demands of school also tend to be visible. Other forms of human conflict, such as that between teenagers and societal mores, religious values, and family traditions can be subtler. And then, the biggest battles of all, the ones that are waged inside our patients, can be hardest or near impossible to see. Conflicts come in all shapes and sizes. All of them are not just welcome to therapy but each is fair and necessary game for the success of therapy.

INVITE CONFLICT INTO THE OFFICE

As a supervisor of psychologists in training, I've observed a fascinating and repeated phenomenon. Young therapists will describe walking to the waiting room to find their patients and their parent(s) in the middle of some brouhaha. In detail they'll relate how a teenager pulled his mother's hair, a father slapped his son, or parents couldn't get their adolescent off the couch. Those trainees will recall the mean, sarcastic, and provocative words that get said, a boy's muttering "You bitch" or a parent's calling to the therapist, "You can have him" as they head to the office.

But it's not what my supervisees witness in itself that catches my attention. We all have homes and families, and have seen enough others to know what they can be like. What intrigues me is what occurs afterward. These clinicians will read me their notes of a teenager's therapy and there'll be no mention of the drama that had taken place minutes earlier in the waiting room or at the end of the previous week's hour. It's as if they've both walked through fireworks or dodged the firemen and hoses outside a burning house, and neither one has said a word about it. What can explain such seemingly unnatural behavior?

That the adolescents themselves don't bring it up isn't surprising. After all, they are adolescents, they ignore all kinds of things.

> *"I went all the way down there in the rain for nothing," a dripping mother says as she takes off her drenched shoes and jacket. "The store wasn't even open." "Oh, yeah," her 15-year-old son replies, buried in a bowl of cereal, "someone called yesterday and said the store will be closed so don't bother coming to work."*

> *A father painting the walls hears someone moving the "Wet Paint" barrels he'd blocked the front door with. "Cripes!" his daughter cries, plowing into the dining room, "I had to climb over trash cans to get in my own house. What are you doing?"*

she asks her father who's holding a paint roller. He looks dis-
approvingly at her backpack. She looks down at the broad
swipe of wet yellow paint across it and screams, "Why did-
n't you put up a sign or something?"

Two upset parents and their teenage son stand in the kitchen.
The mother holds a piece of paper. "How long have you
known about this?" the father asks. Their son looks away.
"It's dated over two weeks ago," adds the mother.

Do any of these snippets bring to mind how long camels can go without drinking? That's how long some teenagers can go without telling their parents anything. Parents can confront their adolescent children with the most incriminating information only to get back a genuine, "Can you give me a ride to Buddy's?" Even caring adolescents can walk out from a documentary on starving Third World children and say nothing but an irritated, "We're not going to eat until *after the dry cleaner?*" Teenagers by nature can be oblivious, self-concerned, and only too happy to talk about something else, if not anything at all.

By now, it's apparent, that sometimes therapists can take the responsibility for raising material that is unavoidable. "Wow, you and your father got some kind of heat going," I've said to an adolescent after walking in on their waiting room skirmish. "What gives with that?" I'll ask a teen who kicks his little sister on his way to the office. Or, sometimes—more and more frequently, the older and more experienced I get—I'll refuse to put a damp blanket on the fire. "Why don't you both come in," I'll say to an angry mother and daughter, using that moment in vivo to gain immediate access to a significant and dynamic piece of family life. More times than not, my merely asking, "Do you actually live like this?" is sufficient to bring chuckles and dis-

cussion. So long as I'm fair with both parties and my intervention proves helpful, my teen patients don't complain about my
bringing up the obvious. They can even come to start doing
it themselves.

ADDRESS DEEP AND PROJECTED
SELF-HATRED

Blatant conflict between a patient and another person can
sometimes be easily resolved. Having their side of the story
heard may be enough for teenagers to examine their contribu-
tions to a situation and to problem solve some peacemaking.
More often, our teenage patients' conflicts with others, especially with family members, run too deep and are too pervasive
for handy resolution. Lincoln's ran as crooked and below the
surface as veins in an Appalachian coal mine.

Prior to meeting me, Lincoln had been evaluated at three
of Boston's prominent teaching hospitals. His parents had sent
me a thick manila envelope full of reports that diagnosed him
as possibly having schizophrenia, depression, bipolar illness, attention deficit, paranoia, oppositional and conduct disorders,
pervasive developmental disability, enuresis, mixed learning
problems, and more. When I read the reports, and saw the
near-laughable and exhaustive lists of diagnoses, I thought it'd
have been easier if they'd simply stated the disorders that Lincoln didn't have. They may have been confused as to what to
call him, but what a damning burden they'd dropped on his parents. Those hospitals had recommended long-term residential
programs and made dire predictions. His parents sought a third
evaluation from a therapist in their community. He met Lincoln
and determined that the first two reports were amiss. He saw the

boy as autistic, though he agreed that outpatient treatment would be a waste of time. A trusted pediatrician finally referred Lincoln's parents to me for a last try.

When I met Lincoln, I could see how he'd baffled evaluators. He was suspicious and sensitive, distractible, impulsive, depressed, hyperanxious, provocative, and defiant along with displaying psychoticlike thought and speech. The facts of his home and school life were dismal. He harbored suicidal fantasies and his aggression was growing violent. And yet, four compelling observations hit me on the head: his great pain; formidable intellect; clear if eccentric cry for help; and, nuclear-proportioned focus on his sister, Paula, two years younger.

"She'd be the Intergalactic Empress, ruler of multiple solar systems," Lincoln explained, agitated.

"And where would you be?" I asked.

"I'd be working in the Martian foundry, forging molten metal to build trinkets for the Empress." Lincoln's hands tightened into fists.

"Trinkets?"

"Unnecessary things to suit her whimsy."

"Isn't Mars kind of a hot place to put a metal forge?"

"Ah," he said with understatement, "that's the point. Where would you propose putting a living hell, on the coast of Maine?" Lincoln's keen wit would prove to be an asset throughout his therapy, and life, and reassured me that at least one foot was standing in this world.

"It's really quite fascinating, if one cares to consider the mathematical possibilities and is not too loathe to question the assumptions carrying these theories," he went on as if he were some mad professor. He chuckled sadistically. "She, she who is celebrated exudes a fulsome odor that pollutes the heav-

ens. Its source, the pus-filled boils that cover her body. But they seem not to notice. They hold her up as their queen nonetheless. And as for me . . ." Lincoln looked out the window. "I am left to slave in the foundry, serving a Goddess whom I detest."

Lincoln grew silent. If not for the palpable darkness of Lincoln's mood, the weight of his words, and that he'd physically hurt his sister, this scene might have been curiously entertaining. It was dead serious.

"Boy, you are some kind of jealous," I noted.

"Why do you say that?" Lincoln asked, coming to earth.

"I don't know. Maybe because you see the world, no scratch that, you see a world bigger than our world that adores her despite all of her flaws. And you, they judge, are worthy of nothing better than . . .

"Cleaning her Majesty's feet?"

I nodded.

Week after week, Lincoln made bits of progress in his relationship with his sister. As he did, his talk of her grew less fantastic and more based on this earth, as in his complaining about how her artistic talents preoccupied the household or how their parents cared more about her emotional needs. His conflict with his younger brother was not so accessible.

Lincoln intimidated and cruelly teased Bennie, a 6-year-old boy half his size. Lincoln would block Bennie's way in the hall or pick him up and not put him down. On a few occasions he'd hurt Bennie badly, and then got even angrier for his brother's being so weak. Although Lincoln was a high school freshman, he could not be left home alone with his younger brother. Lincoln's hatred for Bennie seemed bottomless and seemed to indicate his own removal from the family. "It'll be his fault," Lincoln said sternly.

For months, Lincoln's feelings for Bennie consumed his therapy. Lincoln spent hours destroying his brother in creatively hostile fantasy. He'd design complex Rube Goldberg-inspired devices of torture that he used to sadistically punish a Playmobil plastic child designated to be Bennie. He created doll house scenes that resulted in Bennie's abandonment and orphaning by a family that hated him—"You're ugly, small, stupid, psychotic." Lincoln's play family felt no remorse in letting Bennie know exactly why they kicked him out. That Lincoln used the little Bennie for months, and that he carefully hid "him" between sessions, underscored the profound meaning this play held. But even after Lincoln shelved the little, plastic Bennie, his obsession with his brother continued.

> "The little shit is so pathetic," Lincoln ranted. "He needs my mother to spoon feed him. He walks around the house holding her skirt. Why doesn't she just put a big diaper on him?" Lincoln stuck his finger in his throat and pretended to gag. "I'd like to put him on a raft and push him out into the ocean. I wish an alien race would abduct him to study. He'd make some alien a good pet."

Lincoln's abuse of Bennie dwindled; his preoccupation with the younger boy did not. Lincoln used hour after hour to rip his brother to shreds. I'd ask Lincoln about school and he'd ridicule his brother's physical appearance. I noted Lincoln's frustration with himself for having blown a conversation with a girl he liked, and he verbally decimated Bennie for being a "social retard." Flunk a test and Bennie was an asshole. Sprain an ankle and Bennie was a midget.

> "He's responsible for everything bad in the world . . . the rain, earthquakes, the plagues, everything," Lincoln said.

"Everything?"

"Everything."

"Even my athlete's foot?" I asked.

Lincoln stopped. He looked at my shoes.

"Yeah, that too," he replied with a smile.

Lincoln was getting it, meaning he was gaining awareness of how much he needed Bennie to hate, to blame, to survive.

"Bennie is a trash can for everything bad in your life."

"Blah, blah, blah," Lincoln sang over my words.

"You'd rather talk about Bennie than yourself."

"Blah, blah, blah."

"He's stupid, smelly, shitty, socially retarded, selfish, un-popular, clumsy . . .

Lincoln nodded with pleasure.

". . . hated by your family . . ."

Lincoln's nods slowed.

". . . and deserving to die."

Lincoln quieted.

"He should just kill himself and get it over with, isn't that what you said?"

Lincoln closed his eyes as if trying not to be there.

"Because no one loves him and no one will miss him."

Lincoln covered his ears and hung his head.

"It's too late, Lincoln," I said gently. "You know who you are really talking about, who you really hate."

Lincoln cradled his head with his arms, tears fell on his lap, and he nodded.

In my experience therapy does not occur in bolts of lightning. What appear to be epiphanies of startling insight and emotional purging are actually endpoints of a piece of ongoing work that is culminating in that therapeutic instant. Had I said these words to Lincoln a year, months, or even weeks before, they'd have mostly shut him down.

Through his play and talk, Lincoln came to see what had been obvious since the beginning. Lincoln hated and wanted to destroy himself. Self-contempt that was too much to bear spilled over in his relationships with his sister and more so, his brother. Only self-contempt could account for the depth, intensity, and unrelenting nature of his hateful preoccupation with Bennie. Preoccupying conflict with his brother was far preferable to conflict with himself. Were Lincoln to have experienced his self-dislike more directly, he'd have had to destroy himself. He could not have taken it.

From that moment, Lincoln's therapy grew easier. He came in and talked about the realities of his daily life, taking both credit and blame where due, as well as accepting some parts of life as the fluky turns of fortune that they were. His relationship with his brother improved, though Bennie held a lot of resentment for the years of mistreatment, and that wasn't going to disappear overnight. Best of all, Lincoln took his therapy to a new plane on which he now could come in to talk—*about himself.*

FOCUS ON AMBIVALENCE

Some of us are wholly tortured by ambivalence that never rests and pervades every decision we make. Should I have vanilla or chocolate, marry Gladys or Estelle, be a farmer or an actor? Should I buy or rent, walk or drive, quit or stay? I want both, what do I do? Ambivalence can guarantee my never being happy or content, for I will always wonder whether I should have chosen otherwise. For many, the act of choosing ever incurs anxiety and regret, for choosing A requires that you give up B. Most of us wish we could have it all; some of us actually devote ourselves to trying to attain it all. And that's not good.

Internal conflict is tricky stuff. It helps us to behave and be moral; it can also cause neurotic behavior and suffering. The inner tension of mixed feelings can torment teenagers, especially good boys and girls with a strong conscience (i.e., the part of the body, as someone anonymously once said, that hurts when the rest of us feels good). They want to be models of morality even as they obsess about sex every waking and sleeping hour. They protest against materialism as they drive to the mall for a shopping spree. They want to see themselves as honest but really need that (cheating) A in biology. They struggle to hold onto images of their own perfection while perpetually seeing ways they fall short. Karen Horney beautifully and clearly wrote about the ways that our ideal images of what we should be clash with who we really are, causing a lot of pain and dysfunction. Adolescence is the time when these tensions of character start to take hold.

Therapy has its limitations but it can be adept at helping teenagers face their inner conflict. By allowing himself to be both an observer and available other, the therapist offers the adolescent an unconscious object to displace part of his conflict onto. You, not your patient's conscience, becomes the prude who won't cut his sexy wishes a break. You, not her, think she's lazy for not working in school. It can be so much easier to battle a force outside of yourself than within.

"I'm so confused. Should I go out with Mark and not tell Andy, or should I just be glad I have a boyfriend who likes me?

"You said you don't like Andy like a boyfriend."

"So you think I should go out with Mark?"

"I didn't say that. I was just repeating what you'd said."

"But if I date Mark, Andy will be hurt and I'll look bad."

"What a hard choice. Go out with Mark and look bad or look good with a boy you don't really want to date."

"So you think I'm a slut. I knew it, that's what everyone's going to think."

As the old joke goes, wear one of the two ties a mother gives you and she'll ask why you didn't like the other one. So goes inner conflict, up and down like a turbo-powered seesaw. By steadily helping our teen patients notice their ambivalent and competing feelings, they begin to integrate them. No one is without mixed feelings. The goal is to get along with them well enough to live as freely and free of misery as possible.

I've tried to present a sampling of conflict of varying intensity and circumstance. Of course, conflict comes in an infinite array of sizes, shapes, and color between and within adolescents. No therapeutic schema or plan can anticipate each and every form that conflict will take. With practice and reflection, however, therapists should grow more skilled and adept in recognizing conflict and knowing what to do with it.

9

YOU TALKING TO ME?

Confronting Patients in Therapy

"Yo, I'm talking to you!" "Go ahead, make my day!" We
tend to think of confrontation as yelling in somebody's
face or pushing it into a plate of mashed potatoes. When facing tough teenagers, tough love can appear the way to go. Yet,
new studies suggest that even tough love boot camps may fail
to get through to such youth. The teenage children who come
to us because of violence, law breaking, and defiance have already been confronted plenty. Parents, police, and judges bigger and rougher than we are have confronted these children
to little avail. Nor have the punishing and self-depriving consequences of their misbehaviors taught these wayward adolescents much. Drawing a line in the sand or pinning a patient
up against the wall by his neck may work for cinematic therapists; it probably won't for those of us who practice in the real
world. Therapists must rely on the power of their words, behaviors, and presence to confront the adolescents they treat.

What does it mean to confront someone? *Webster* defines the
verb *confront* as "bringing face to face," as when the little pigs
open their peephole to see the hungry wolf. What does it mean
to confront someone *therapeutically*? It involves the creation of

conditions in which our patients are brought to face some meaningful conflict in the complex matrix of their thinking, feeling, or behavior. The ultimate and ideal confrontation does not pit patient against parent, teacher, or therapist as much as it compels the adolescent to meet some challenge within. How, in everyday practice with teens, does a therapist best foster those conditions and utilize them for the therapy's sake?

CONFRONT IN SMALL DOSES

This kind of problem ever floors me in its presentation. It goes something like this:

> *Teen: "Everyone sucks. My history teacher gave me a C on the report that I busted my ass on. Samantha got a B+ and her paper wasn't as good. She's such a little kiss ass. Then the study monitor gave me a detention for throwing a paper airplane at her. It was Thompson, the asshole never gets caught."*

Such a teen may go on to diss his mother, father, brothers, and sisters, and half the population of Springfield without a shred of awareness that he is at odds with virtually every person in his life. Gee, let's see, what is the one common denominator of all of these injustices? While the answer is obvious, blurting it out may send the adolescent scurrying or, at best, our words may fall with an empty thud.

I find that helping teenagers process their conflicts bit by bit allows them to make sense of and manage one piece of a puzzle, where the whole puzzle would undoubtedly overwhelm them. But first we must make note of all that we hear.

Remarks such as "Man, what a day!" or "Gee, everyone has it out for you?" efficiently convey that we have heard their pleas. Even a career criminal can feel persecuted by the immense grief he's given, regardless of whether deserved or not. Our empathic reaction to his side of the story may even lead to some confessions of his own. "I wonder why everyone has it out for you" may go a little farther, expressing comparable acceptance while fishing for more. The child's replying, "Because I'm a fucked-up butt-head" will encourage us more than his "because they're assholes" or "because I'm smarter than they are."

Once the child's misery is heard, we can do a little more confrontation.

"Is that the paper you said you were going to piss together on on the way home from therapy last week?" ["Yeah, but it came out pretty good."] "Do you have it with you?" [Teen pulls out crumpled and sloppy paper covered with careless spelling, half-finished sentences, and the blackened smudges of wild erasures. "I guess it's not my best work ever."] "What was Samantha's paper on?" ["Uh, I actually didn't see, but she always gets good grades 'cause the teacher likes her better.] "You got a detention and you never even threw an airplane." ["Oh, I threw one but it missed her head. Thompson's hit her shoe." Teen laughs.]

I made up these examples for the purpose of this discussion. But, be assured, they represent what my most common hours with teenagers sound like. I try to bump the child where he is at each juncture, pointing my observation and curiosity just enough to confront the unspoken. It frequently works like magic, as with one boy who told me with pride and pleasure

how he'd humiliated a girl in his class. My simply and nonjudg-
mentally noting how he'd enjoyed doing it evoked feelings of
shame and regret that caught him off guard. It is a rare moment
when this technique doesn't apply.

Beware though, that it may not be as easy as it sounds. Therapists' perpetual parroting soon grows tiring and off-putting.
We must think actively how best to pursue each snippet of experience to create the right mix of understanding and wonder
as to stir the child's tentative equilibrium, empowering the
adolescent to confront more and more of what he really feels
and does. And best of all, though the therapist is the medium
that helps bring this material forth, it is teenagers' own words
that confront them. By the end of that hypothetical hour,
there's a good chance that the boy who felt mistreated by the
world would have begun to see that he himself might play a
leading role in the injustice he's suffered.

Gradually, this work will create enough room for some mutual problem solving. "I wonder, is there anything you can do
to get on your teacher's good side?" "What can you do to get
along with an asshole like that?" "Any way you can convince
your boss he can trust you at the register?" This process will
go slowly, but it will go, and may benefit from our guidance and
education as to possibilities and strategies to help teenagers
see others' perspectives, the missing links that causes many of
their conflicts with people.

CONFRONT REPETITIVE SIGNS
OF RESISTANCE

Adolescents often find it consciously or unconsciously difficult
to face certain aspects of themselves and their lives. We ask

them about their problems and misbehaviors. Instead of the clear and accountable answers we look for, we instead get diversions, deflections, and distractions. It would be wild analysis to aggressively pursue every pregnant pause, twitch, daze, and change of subject. When they happen time and again, however, they mandate that the therapist do something, even if it is something gentle.

Andrew was referred to me in the sixth grade after he'd pushed a classmate through the glass trophy display in his middle school's foyer. Two teachers and the principal reportedly had to pull Andrew off the other boy as they wrestled in the broken glass. Andrew's assault had shocked everyone, especially its ferocity. Andrew was a slim and not very physical boy.

> *"He kept calling me Andrea," Andrew said with considerable discomfort. "I don't like saying it but it's the only way I can explain why I did it."*

I later learned that Andrew had never told the school the reason for his losing control. He felt too embarrassed that the kids had teased him "for being a girl." "Besides," he'd added, "they don't like me there anyway." Andrew meant his teacher.

I called Andrew's teacher. She told me that despite his meek demeanor, he'd use his superior intelligence like a weapon to critique other students' work. She described Andrew's report on Jefferson and how he had purposely, so she thought, used big words that the other children wouldn't understand. "He seems to enjoy making them look foolish," she said. When I couldn't help but note her growing anger, she confessed that he'd also challenged her competence, pointing out when she misspoke or got facts wrong. "He puts us all off," she said.

"I haven't a clue," Andrew said. He'd been wondering aloud why his peers seemed to have it out for him. "I don't bug them," he said, and I didn't question him. "I mind my own business."

I asked Andrew what school was like in general. He came alive and told stories of how boring it was, how not into learning the other kids were, and how little his teacher knew.

"Do they know how you feel, Andrew?"

"I don't know," he said. "I don't know." His mood subdued and I saw something in him that I'd never seen and haven't seen since with any other child or grown-up. A thin, bright red line circled each eye. "Anyway," he rebounded, "I'm going skiing tomorrow." The circles disappeared.

Andrew parents were concerned, as one might guess. His mother, a quiet and thoughtful woman, felt heartbroken to see her child treated this way. She in no way endorsed his aggression and yet felt deeply for his feeling so attacked. Andrew's father, an impressively bright man, chastised the school while, at the same time, expressing distress with his son. "I don't understand what he's done to get a whole school to dislike him. And now, since he jumped on that kid," he went on, "they're calling Andrew 'crazed.'"

Hour by hour, Andrew shared more details about his frustrations with classmates and his teacher. Each time he'd own a little more of his difficulties. "Maybe she was upset," he said, when considering why a new girl had joined in with the teasing.

"About what?" I asked.

Andrew couldn't reply. As had become ritual whenever painful thoughts arose, he'd squint, stop talking, and those

*red circles would appear. Red circles always signaled the
end of a discussion.*

The flames roared at school and yet Andrew spoke more
about home. "I've got to rewrite a paper tonight. My Dad doesn't
think it's ready"; "My Dad was right. It was selfish of me to
eat the last slice of bacon"; "I won't be going on the outing. I
never raked the leaves and my father's frustrated with me." Red
circles, red circles, red circles.

It was the fall and Andrew had made much progress. He was
in a new school and had become a more generous and kindly
classmate. He thrived academically and was blossoming athletically. But he still had too many moments of what appeared
to be excruciating discomfort accompanied by red circles and
an inability to talk. These, he said, were starting to happen
at home in his room, even when alone, and he hated them. "I
don't know what they are," he'd say with greater and greater
frustration. Understanding and relief would soon come.

*Andrew sat in the overstuffed armchair opposite my own. His
father sat in a smaller chair to the side.*

*His father told stories about Andrew's recent accomplish-
ments, but each one somehow implied a failing. As his father
spoke, Andrew grew paler and stiffer.*

*"What's the matter?" his father asked several times, grow-
ing annoyed and demanding. "This is your therapy. You can
talk too!" Andrew squinted. Red circles jumped out. "You
can say anything, I don't mind," his father prodded. Andrew
pulled inward. The red circles got narrower and brighter.*

It was a terribly painful standoff.

"I give up." His father smacked his hand on my desk.

*"I think Andrew doesn't feel he can say what he wants,"
I said.*

*"So why doesn't he just cry," his father said, looking to me.
"Why doesn't he just cry, damn it!"*

*"Because you told me not to!" Andrew screamed out in a
broken sob. "That's why." Andrew turned and buried his
head in the chair.*

*"Oh, shit," Andrew's father said, his own eyes tearing.
He slammed his palms against his forehead. "You're talking about the fourth grade, aren't you?" Andrew nodded.
"You stupid, stupid man." He dropped his head into his
hands.*

*When Andrew composed himself, his eyes were puffy and
wet but the red circles were gone. He described an incident at
school in which a soccer ball had hit his face and he'd cried.
His father, Andrew recalled, had told him sternly to never
cry again for that was weak and like a girl and that he
would get teased for it.*

*"It's all your fault," Andrew said, perhaps the first time
he'd ever confronted his father. "You're always disappointed
with me."*

*Andrew stared at his father. He was not about to let him
off the hook.*

*"Maybe I should meet with Dr. Bromfield to see why I'm so
tough on everyone," his father finally. Andrew agreed, adding
that his father might also wonder why he's so hard on himself. They walked out in a side-to-side hug.*

A small moment, being told not to ever cry again, had
imprinted itself onto Andrew's psyche. Andrew indeed had
stopped crying. The sadness that had preceded that incident,
however, had not vanished, and only grew larger as Andrew's

crying, feeling, and grieving were halted. Red circles were the only clue to the grief that lay dormant and unexpressed. My persistent and patient confrontation of those circles not only led to Andrew expressing himself more fully; it eventually empowered him to himself confront his father for that one event as well as for a lifetime of criticism and disapproval. Although new areas of resistance arose, they always will, I never saw those red circles again.

CONFRONT TEENAGERS' INTERNAL BATTLES

Confronting inner turmoil is key to the majority of cases and vignettes presented throughout the book. It's where it all ends up, or begins, or more accurately, where it lives day in and day out. These are the conflicts that pervade every nook and cranny of adolescents, running from their frontal lobes down to their big toes, influencing their every thought, feeling, and action. Conflicts with the outside can be discrete. Avoid that jerk down the hall and you're carefree. But inner conflicts are everywhere for, as has become a psychological cliché, wherever you go, you go too.

Consider a college student who'd come to me depressed with migraines. She'd been to migraine clinics in Boston and in Cleveland, MRIs, CAT scans, and other tests had found nothing. She'd tried several medications, some with significant side effects, but with mediocre results.

"I'd do anything to get rid of these," she said, having told me about the years of frustrating visits to doctors and hospitals. But when I told her about a visualizing exercise that had

lessened migraine pain for some of my patients, she declined,
saying that day wasn't a good time to try something new.

How does one understand that? Someone suffers great pain,
and spends a great deal of time, money, and effort seeking medical help. I suggest something easy she can try for 10 minutes
or so in the cushy chair she's sitting in, with a guarantee that it
will neither hurt nor have side effects, and might even relieve
her headache, and she says, thanks anyway.

Our answer came months later. A migraine had followed an
enormously frustrating phone call. But she said there was no
use in talking about it, for it was hopeless, there was no solution. That was the key. Her migraines, we discovered, came
when she couldn't stand to think what she was thinking. The
horrible pain immobilized her thoughts. "Nothing moves in
my head during a migraine," she described, "as if my head is
constipated." As she grew able to tolerate her thoughts and
feelings, her migraines diminished, and she came to compre-
hend why she'd been stuck. She'd been in a relationship in
which she felt stuck. Talking and thinking about it would have
made her make a choice: leave or stay. And she wasn't ready for
that. Subsequent therapy and work on her dependent nature
led to her breaking off that relationship and finding new and
healthier ones. Her insufferable migraines devolved into less
frequent, less severe headaches.

Inner conflict can exist between two wishes, what someone wants and what they do, what they say and what they do,
what they want to see and what is, who they want to be and
who they are. Internal conflict can exist between impulse and
self-control, as in a teenager's wish for nasty sex and a competing wish to be good or a fear of AIDs and STDs. Or, it can
arise between the perfect me a child dreams of being and the

imperfect being she cannot humanly help but be. Or, between the *I should be's* (*loved, in charge, self-sufficient* . . .) that, as the underappreciated Karen Horney so clearly wrote, can tyrannically rule a person, producing harmful conflict, self-hatred, and aspects of a false self.

"You say all you want are C grades, but you stay up until past midnight every night studying." "You say you aren't jealous, but you spent 40 minutes putting her down." "You want to just belong and you want to be the Queen of everything and everybody." When spoken gently, kindly, at the right time, and most of all, for the genuine welfare of the child, such confrontations can lead adolescents toward relief, stability, and growth they never dreamed possible.

As was true for the previous chapter and its focus on conflict, this discussion of confrontation in therapy is meant to be more impressionistic and evocative than exhaustive or systematic. Does the therapist speak loud or soft, talk at length or briefly, crowd in on patients or back off? Does he comment today or wait until he sees the same pattern repeat itself several times? Does he push or wait for his patients to do so for themselves? Yes, again it's true, there is no one answer. But that doesn't leave it up to happenstance or risky I'm-with-ya baby kinds of doing therapy. Thinking about our work, as in this chapter, can help inform and ground therapists, enhancing the likelihood that their intuitions and interventions meet the clinical mark.

10

WORK IT!

Keeping Teens Working at Therapy

P hysical fitness is a boom industry. Health clubs are on every corner, the exercise machines in gyms get fancier, and anyone who watches daytime television has seen the endless parade of home conditioning gadgets and videos. New and improved ways of steeling abs and dieting have become a daily staple of newspapers, men's and women's magazines, and television talk shows. Even the findings of medical science, once confined to journals and scientific conferences, regularly fly through the media to report the benefits of vitamin E or walking uphill versus downhill. And yet, for all this hoopla and who knows how many trillions of dollars for its research, design, manufacturing, advertising, and media coverage, there are actually only two essential truths to fitness: consume no more calories than you burn, and second, challenge your body and its muscles just enough to make them work a little harder. These indisputable and clear principles, known forever, are all anyone needs to know.

While comparing therapy to physical exercise has its limitations, consider how it applies. Doesn't much of life require practice and use? Spending more time with people advances our social skills. Learning ways to cope and compensate overcomes learning problems. Taking courses in home or auto repair can enhance a sense of independence just as repeated writing can enhance our ability to express ourselves in words. But the relevance of the exercise analogy extends beyond pragmatic skills to more basic capacities for human functioning.

Children who sometimes have to wait, learn to wait, be patient, and delay gratification. Learning to work and succeed without moment-by-moment rewards and applause fosters genuine self-esteem and a healthy work ethic. Being held accountable for their behaviors, and being incrementally allowed to sort through the confusing dilemmas of life, strengthens children's moral strength and wisdom. Likewise, experiencing tough moments and circumstances, seeing that they can rise above the trips and thorns life throws their way, fortifies children's egos and resilience and lends them a confidence that they can handle life.

Somewhat like a gym for the psyche, the therapy office can be the place for the adolescent to exercise life skills and ego strengths. There, our teenage patients can learn proper techniques to take with them back into the world so they continue their exercise programs. As important, they will have a trusted trainer who will help to keep them on track, take note of and share pride in their gains, and who will ever confirm the worth of their efforts. As a supervisor told me early in training, little good in life comes easy. So it is with therapy.

CREATE A WORKING ENVIRONMENT

I once worked with a therapist whose patients loved coming to see her, and she never told the rest of the staff. We'd often see her patients walking down the hall with flowers, gift bags, bottles of wine, and the like. If we happened to catch her welcoming or saying good-bye to a patient, we were sure to see a hug or hear a parting recommendation for a movie or a see-you-there kind of remark. And the laughter that came from that office seemed more like a comedy club. At the day's end she'd wonder, with some oblivious sunshine, how come her colleagues looked drained.

The rest of us, all trainees with an ample lack of experience and no dearth of self-doubt, wondered what we were doing wrong. Yes, sometimes our patients joked and laughed, and once in a while they brought us something. But our therapies seemed so much messier. Our patients seemed to have mixed feelings about coming, they loved *and* hated it. They often left us angry, confused, frustrated, saddened, all sorts of feelings from the negative end of the feeling spectrum.

Over time, though, we discovered things. At case conferences we heard about shared jokes and proclamations of attachment, but little else. "What about her drinking?" the clinic director would ask. "It never came up" that clinician answered. When describing child cases, she'd talk of how they played out elaborate scenes of fancy that seemed to vanish into thin air. And, as time went on, even she complained that her patients didn't stay in therapy long. They would leave, she said, saying that therapy wasn't doing much for them but they hoped the two of them could be friends.

Since that time, my experience—doing it, supervising it, reading about it, being in it—has taught me that all good cheer and feeling does not a sound therapy make. Not that good feeling does not have its virtues. To feel warmth, appreciated, and just plain liked by your therapist can be healing and counter toxic self-dislike, especially for patients who feel unloved by their own families. A therapy that has to stay at that level, however, risks becoming a be-happy room that bars any other kinds of feeling. Love can sometimes be the answer, but positive regard in itself won't usually ease deep-seated hurts and inner turmoil. While nurturing a strong connection is paramount, adolescents are not in therapy to have us as friends (though they may experience it as such). They are there because they need our professional help. They are there to work.

GRAB MOMENTS OF
THERAPEUTIC POTENTIAL

Uri wanted friends dearly and would send me e-mails signed, "Your Friend." He wanted much more from me, however.

> *This was about my eighth hour with Uri, a seventh grader diagnosed with Asperger's syndrome. He presented as a supremely intelligent, verbal, and anxious child. Throughout our beginning hours, he'd start and stammer, oftentimes forgetting what he wanted to say, or distracting himself to confusion. Enabled by loose joints, he would fold his hands, then invert and curl them while wrapping his legs tightly together and squeezing. He looked like a human twisted cruller doing isometrics.*
> *"It makes me feel more relaxed," he explained.*

Uri went to a small school. Although he liked some of his peers and wanted good friends, he found himself alone a lot in the classroom, on the playground, and after school. He said he didn't mind because it gave him more time to work on his novel, an ambitious science fiction epic traversing multiple civilizations and millenia.

> *"It combines the chimeric powers of the unicorn and the dolphin, while able to read minds across solar systems. Being comfortable in both water and on land, it is the counterpower to face the evils of the other worlds."*
>
> I tried to follow but it wasn't easy. Uri had spent the better part of many of those hours telling in infinite detail about the creatures he was creating for that novel, a work that he estimated would exceed a thousand pages.
>
> *"The dolphins follow from the mythos of Delphi, though some say. . . ."*
>
> I marveled at what Uri told me. The enormous effort of his inventing and writing such a complicated fantasy world had to represent something extraordinarily meaningful and psychologically useful to him, not to mention the sheer act of doing that much writing.
>
> As Uri spoke, he repeatedly cleared his throat and coughed. He'd also visibly gulp. "Dr. Bromfield, do you think I should place the dolphins at the Temple of Syros or would it better to let them migrate through space?"
>
> "Uri . . ."
>
> "I know what you're thinking." He laughed. "You don't think that dolphins can fly. Well, they can't really fly. They . . ."
>
> "Uri!" I said. "It's almost . . ."
>
> "I know, time's up and I didn't leave a second for you to talk. That's rude, I agree." My intrusion had shaken Uri. He deliberately and awkwardly sat straight on the edge of his chair, held his head up high, and forced his eyes to face me. It was obvious how hard and unnatural it must have felt to prepare himself to listen to what I was about to say.

"Uri." Uri squinted and blinked and slid back in his chair.

"I'm sorry," he said, rigidly getting back into what position.

"All I wanted to say is your story is so complex and rich."

Uri smiled and his eyes teared. "Most people can't stand listening to it and they walk away or their eyes glaze over."

I looked to the clock, we were over time.

"I know, I know," Uri said as he jumped up and held his hand out to shake as had become our custom. "Thanks for listening and for telling me how rude I can be." Uri marched through the door.

"Hey," I called to him, "come back here." Uri hustled in and I gestured for him to sit back down. "You're not going to get away with that," I said. Uri chuckled, intrigued. "Did I say you were rude?" I asked.

Uri smiled. "No, I did, but I know I was monologuing and that's rude."

"I believe you can monologue and that maybe sometimes it can be rude," I went on. "But today you weren't anything like rude." Uri sighed in relief. "I'm your therapist and you've been trying your best to share your world with me. And that world includes Mythodonia!" Uri nodded his head in hearty agreement, then like a reflex launched back into his novel.

"Gotta go," I said, pointing to the clock. Uri grabbed my hand, shook it again, and walked out with a jaunty step.

A curious therapist could have seen many places to jump in. The anxious mannerisms, the one-way monologue, the interesting creatures, the writing of a novel. And he well might have turned any of those to therapeutic profit. Recognizing his nuclear-sized anxiety and the compulsion of his story-telling,

I did not want to overdo it. Push such children too hard and they are apt to withdraw. Yet, to let him go out into the night with his self-critical misunderstanding felt wrong. He'd have gone home believing that he'd been bad and that his therapist had confirmed that. We could get more done that day, I knew, and the faster I could alleviate his suffering, the better.

In rather a short time, Uri stopped his monologues, replacing them with real discussions about the ways that being with other teens stressed, perplexed, and discouraged him. As his ability to listen and attune to others slowly grew, so did his interactions. And best of all, rather than ditch his novel, he embraced it more, as his mother, the world's best advocate, found Uri a real novelist to mentor Uri in his fiction writing. She, as do many parents, saw the virtue in grabbing moments of potential at home, also.

GET THE MOST OUT OF THERAPY'S WORK

I don't mean to scare you. My concept is probably the geometry of therapy, or maybe just the algebra of it. Bear with me.

Imagine a basic graph, as follows:

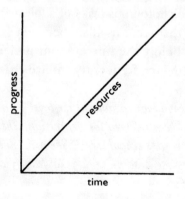

Think of the bottom corner where all three lines join as the beginning of therapy. The adolescent starts off with a certain amount of ego, self-esteem, resilience, and tolerance. Let's call those *resources*. Over *time*, as therapy proceeds, and *progress* accrues, the teenager's resources grow (upward). At any one instant in time in therapy, the teenager's resources lie somewhere along that line. That is where the power of therapy lies, where much of the work occurs. The space below the line is comfortable, like going to the gym and lifting too little weight. The space above the line is overwhelming, more like weights that will strain or even tear our psychic and emotional joints. Ideally, we want therapy to travel along that line of tension, working our teen patients to the maximum that they can ably handle.

What actually occurs at that line can be conceptualized in various ways. It's the place where the patient feels enough pain or anxiety to face something, or the place where they care enough to change. It can be viewed as the place where they can sufficiently cope with a devastating memory without being retraumatized. It can represent a place that balances adolescents' wishes to please others versus their wish to do what they want. And it can serve as the point of tension that lies between all of those tortuously dichotomous tasks of adolescence, the highly ambivalent poles that teens oscillate between.

Grow too lazy below the line and our patients fade away. Head above the line too frequently and we chase them away.

"Would you like to look around at the toys?" I asked the 13-year-old who'd been referred for depression. She drew beautiful flowers. "What's school like?" She drew flowers. "How about drawing me a scene with your family doing something?" Flowers.

Francine was one of my first private practice patients. I was clinically apprehensive about going out on my own and worried about making a living. She'd been referred by a popular pediatrician in a nearby town. I wanted to do well by her for all kinds of reasons. Week after week, I'd stand on my head trying to engage Francine in talk, play, anything. But week after week, she only drew and she drew only flowers.

Each hour I'd push and push, getting little back and frustrating both of us. Each time Francine left, I'd beat myself up for having blown it. Just to let her be was the answer, I knew. But I couldn't help myself. I felt so unhelpful and impotent. Finally, her parents canceled her hour, permanently. "She finds it too stressful," they explained.

Of course, no therapy spends most of its time right along that line; in fact, a lot of therapy prepares the child for those more occasional times when the psychic planets align. Francine had needed a therapist to nurture and help prepare her for that in a way that I hadn't. It is rare that we as therapists hit the bullseye, for human tensions shift as quixotically as electrons. And yet, it is the skill and empathy that grows with training, experience, and learning from mistakes that enable therapists to get better at what they do, doing it well enough, enough of the time.

11

WORD UP

Speaking the Patient's Language

Listen to yourself for a day. Hear how differently you speak to your spouse, your children, your friends, and your boss. You speak tenderly here but sternly there. It's second nature: You alter the tenor, loudness, pace, and vocabulary of what you say to suit the immediate relationship or circumstance facing you. Even your vocabulary, while mostly a constant, adapts to the context of your conversation. Your interruptions, sarcastic asides, and skeptical glances enrich and add meaning to these interactions, like artistic embellishments to a watercolor. And then there are the prolific misunderstandings. Watch how others react to what you say, sensing, correctly or not, that you are being critical, angry, irritated, or sarcastic. Think also of the reverse, how often what others say stings you. *How could you say that? What did you mean? What's your point?* Misunderstanding is essential to daily communication, and frequently leads to misreading the wrong meaning or motive into another's words.

These aspects of human conversation can be even more intense in therapy. After all, as sociologists have written, the therapeutic relationship can be one of imbalance where a vulnerable patient seeks the help of a powerful therapist. Even when they do not show it, adolescent patients are likely to hear acutely what their therapists say to and about them. The therapist's words can wield great influence, for good and bad. How can therapists use language to their teenage patients' best advantage?

TALK PLAIN ENGLISH

It's curious, isn't it, how much psychobabble can turn a person off? I cringe when I hear television therapists ask the person on their couch, *How does it feel?* I myself have never responded well to that question. But it's not our fault. Therapists have often been trained to couch their words in the most careful of terms, using such tentative and qualified phrasing that their patients cannot help but be confused, bothered, and put at a distance. "I wonder if you maybe have been experiencing upset that those girls may have wanted to hurt your feelings?" I might have asked during graduate school when my patient spoke of being cruelly teased. "Ouch, what a bitch!" I've since learned, is the better response.

Therapists can have good reasons for being circumspect, such as a solid appreciation for the impact their words have on patients. But saying it the long way around can make an adolescent wonder what her therapist is saying or if she even hears her. Consider Monica, a tenth-grade girl referred for depression and poor self-esteem.

> *"Look at this." Monica pulled her shirt sleeve up so I could see her upper arm. "I'm so fat," she said, continuing what had been an anguished and 45-minute litany of her inadequacies. "And my legs." She slapped her thigh. "They're fatter."*

> "*Fat, ugly, stupid, mean, selfish, awkward, lazy,*" I
> paused. "*Did I forget anything?*"
>   *Monica held her chin, to feign thinking. "My little toe is
> twisted," she replied.*

I could have spoken of the ways in which Monica was not
even close to the horror she thought herself to be. But her parents, teachers, and friends had done that already, and it hadn't
helped. "They don't see who I really am," Monica would complain. I also could have asked her to reflect on herself, "Do you
really think you are all those things?" But I knew that she did.
And to say, "You feel ugly, stupid . . ." would have avoided her
insistence that she doesn't *imagine* that she's like that, she *is*.
My accurately summarizing all she'd said validated her feelings, but it went a step farther. My tongue-in-cheek invitation
for any last-minute and unspoken faults noted the enormity
of her self-rebuke, implying, with a little humor, there was no
way any one person could be so worthless.

If there's anything one can say about therapists, it's that they
want to relieve people's hurt. Therapists' wish to do everything
to help and nothing to harm can explain their tendency to
avoid more direct comment. Compare these variations on a
theme, therapist remarks to a teenager having difficulty at his
weekend job.

> "*All of these experiences at work could really frustrate a per-
> son.*"
>   "*Teenagers who have experiences like that often feel frus-
> tration.*"
>   "*I wonder if you might be frustrated.*"
>   "*You must be frustrated.*"
>   "*Frustrating!*"

You're right if you are thinking, give me a break, there's no one way to say something. My examples are meant to help us question the implications of what we say: "All of these experiences at work could really frustrate a person." In saying that I miss the intensity of her experience and, to her, am suggesting that a better person would not be frustrated. "Some teenagers who have experiences like that often feel frustration." Ditto, not to mention, who cares what other kids feel? I'm talking about me. "I wonder if you might be frustrated." Blah, blah, blah. "You must be frustrated." Now, you're going to tell me how I have to feel? "Frustrating!" Bingo!

SPEAK DIRECTLY

Of course, there are clinical circumstances when any of those phrasings would work, or when maybe a different one would have worked better. Generally, direct is good. In my supervision work, graduate students training to be therapists have taught me about this. As we go over the notes of the sessions, they often laugh at their own long and wordy sentences. They, so they've told, fear taking firmer stands and committing to their observations or intuitions, even when they feel confident in their perceptions. Young therapists' reluctance to just say it also may attest to their understandable discomfort in knowing how much they mean to their patients, as in this example from my supervision of an advanced psychology trainee.

"Annie gave me another card. I didn't know what to do. I felt so bad."

Karen had been presenting her notes from a session with an 11-year-old teenager adopted in infancy by parents who, in turn, had parented her poorly. In this and the previous two hours, the girl had showered Karen with gifts and gestures that spoke of her affection for the talented young therapist. Annie's love for Karen was easy to grasp. Karen was a kind, dependable, and gentle woman who cared deeply about Annie, maybe the first to do so in the girl's chaotic and traumatic childhood. Karen too had been a staunch advocate for the girl, especially helping to insulate her from her adoptive parents' bitter legal fight for custody.

> *"She just kept making me Valentine cards that said, 'I love you' and then she'd hand me the empty envelopes and the markers, like I was supposed to make her cards." Karen's hands signed her helplessness. "I felt so bad."*
>
> *"So why didn't you?" I asked.*
>
> *"I can't just write, 'I love you.' That would be too confusing. She's an adolescent girl who was abused."*
>
> *I nodded in agreement.*
>
> *"So, what am I supposed to write?" Karen asked, frustrated.*
>
> *I waited.*
>
> *"Dear Annie, You want me to love you like you love me? Is that what I'm supposed to write?" Karen asked with irritation.*
>
> *"You know it is."*
>
> *"But my internship ends in two months," Karen blurted, burying her eyes in her hands. "She needs someone who'll love her for the rest of her life. Not someone who's leaving her!"*

Not only did Karen have the skills to be a fine therapist, she had the heart. Who could argue with her wisdom that Annie deserved lifelong love? But Annie also deserved good therapy to help her grow past the hurt and neglect she'd known for too long in her short life. And Karen was providing that.

> *"I don't want to be that important in a patient's life,"* Karen said.
> *"But you are,"* I said as I handed Karen the tissue box. *"You already are that important."*

Plain English can capture the vividness and intensity of what someone feels in the moment. "You want me to kill you," can be a more loving and confirming response than the more measured and circuitous, "You're experiencing suicidal ideation and would like me to help find you relief. Maybe we should talk about the possibility of a psychopharmacology consultation. . . ." The teenage girl who'd spent an hour talking of her profound self-disgust and wish that I'd put her out of her misery left that hour lighter and less despairing. She knew from my words that I'd gotten the darkness of where she was. She left feeling less alone.

If words are the currency of therapeutic exchange, then therapists want to speak with economy. Striving for clarity and simplicity will insure that our thoughts hit the mark and leave more time for our patients to react. Of course, I am not referring to the kind of therapist silence that tarnished psychoanalyses of old and helped make them poor treatment. Therapists should not hesitate to speak when they have something worthwhile to say. There's no virtue, for sure, in holding back anything that might facilitate growth or relief in the teenager. And yet, as in any setting, those who speak less frequently and with more wisdom tend to be more listened to.

Finally, we remember the power of plain language when it comes to querying our patients. Saying "I don't get it," "I'm sorry but you lost me," or "You must be kidding me?" are all legal, just as "right," "in your dreams," and "not in my lifetime" may be. I typically say, "What was their name?" when patients bring up friends and enemies (actual names makes the description more immediate and build the cast of characters that comprise the teenager's life). I'm surprised to hear trainees not know basic facts about a child's life even after months of treatment. It's not just okay to ask, it's good to ask. And, despite what we were taught, there's always *Why?* and *Why not?*

CREATE A SHARED LANGUAGE

In almost every therapy, the patient and therapist create a special world and language that is theirs alone to share. Like so many boy scouts with secret codes and decoding rings, therapists and their patients have phrases and private jokes, for example, that can efficiently telegraph their communications, saying hundreds of words in a few.

> *"White belt," Karl mumbled, deadpan.*
> *"What?" his mother asked. I smiled at Karl.*
> *"Nothing," Karl replied, "I was just thinking about what you said."*
> *Karl's mother had suggested that her 13-year-old son invite some other boys over to help paint the garage.*
> *"I'll make sandwiches and you boys will have a good time."*

Karl's parents were immigrants from another country who'd had Karl, an only child, later in life. "I don't have more friends because I'm weird and so anxious around people," Karl explained poignantly and accurately. "They think it's like when they were young in their old country." *White belts* became the term Karl used to mean something antiquated, irrelevant, old-fogyish, usually some idea that his loving parents had for making his life better. He'd gotten the idea on vacation in South Florida when he'd seen how many old men wore white belts.

Bitch alert, Headache no. 25, and pretending to strangle his own neck were like-minded keywords used by my teenage patients to speed dial how they felt. It is a rare therapy in which an adolescent patient and I don't share such mutually familiar shortcuts. Oftentimes, our mutual understanding is accomplished by way of analogies or metaphors that make some complex emotion or dynamic sufficiently concrete, palpable, and clarifying. Mark, a junior high student with Asperger's syndrome and a nonverbal learning disability, was especially keen at using language this way, as when he discussed his feelings about girls at school.

> *"Everyone goes for the hot girls. I don't get it. It's like my glasses have special lenses that allow me to see inner beauty. And lots of the times, the hot girls are pretty ugly inside. But there are lots of girls that are lovely people under their skin."*

What an unusual and refreshing perspective, and what a wondrous representation to describe his capacity to see beyond and beneath a person's physical appearance. Mark knew that the way he saw others was not the norm, at least not in his seventh grade class. From that time on he referred to his special lenses when trying to describe some aspect of his perceptions of others. Mark also used analogies freely and spurred me to do the same as, for example, when he'd been told that instead of writing on his laptop during recess and lunchtime, he was to play sports, a mandate that left him feeling more alone and on the outs.

> *"It would be like if the other kids were told that they can't play football and soccer," I suggested.*
> *"Yeah," Mark affirmed, enlivened by my attempt to grasp his predicament. "Only, it's as if they were told that they all had to sit and write stories like I do."*
> *"Then they'd know just what you feel."*
> *"Exactly," Mark replied, smiling with satisfaction.*

Less frequently, I find teenage patients who, rather than employ discrete phrases or literary devices, will use their entire therapy to establish an understanding and framework that they can visit week after week. Think about Graham, a profoundly underachieving and oppositional tenth grader referred because his frustration was turning violent.

> *"Do you wear clothes in your house?" Graham asked with the perfectly straight face and nonchalance that I'd come to expect.*
> *"Usually."*
> *"How do you know if your kidneys are Democrat or Republican?"*
> *"By how they vote."*
> *"Who's your dog's favorite mystery writer? I've been wondering about that lately."*
> *"Conan Doyle, you know Sherlock Holmes,* The Hound of the Baskervilles, *that sort of thing."*

For many, many hours Graham would pelt me with such questions, ranging from the personal to the arcane. Sometimes

I'd just answer, some I'd defer in an attempt to see what he was really asking, most I would get a chuckle from (which made Graham very happy). But almost all of the time we would note how much he enjoyed provoking me and how difficult it was for him to find any other way to be close to me. The understanding that slowly came led to Graham asking a different breed of question dealing with my children, my other patients, his jealousies, and fears about himself.

> *"Hungry man! Hungry man!" Graham sang at the top of his lungs in a deep operatic scream that exploited his deep-barreled chest. As he'd been doing for several weeks, he lay on the floor beside my feet. He held a miniature toy replica of a TV dinner. "I am a hungry man!" he took a huge bucket of Legos and spilled them over his face. "Feed me! Feed me! I am a hungry man!"*

Graham's relentless needs and envy tripped him at every step, obstructing friendships and causing constant battles at home. This regressing play, which he reenacted for many hours, enabled those issues to come to the forefront in a form that, appealing to his awesome sense of humor, he could tolerate and work with. Throughout his treatment, feelings of jealousy or envy were always heralded by his cry of "Hungry man!"

> *His hour was nearing its end, and Graham was stressing out. He'd worked diligently to make an impressive-looking Haz-Mat suit, boots, and helmet from numerous sheets of typing paper taped together. As if that task was not enough, he strove to give his modern outfit a medieval flavor. For the final touches he was building a cardboard sword and shield. "I'm never going to get this done," he said as he worked frenetically*

on the shield while continually retaping ripped seams. When his father came to pick him up, Graham walked outside with his sword and shield held high. "I come to free them!" Graham proclaimed, giving both his father and myself a good laugh.

As Graham's therapy progressed, he spent more of his hours creating impressive symbols of his angst. This play enabled him to work on issues, such as: his judging himself to be uncreative; his reluctance to produce in school; his many fears, including that of germs and terrorism; his feelings about war; and, his inhibited wish to perform in front of others. By anyone's standards, Graham's therapy was a creative marvel. But when you think about it, doesn't every therapist and teen patient create a shared world that grows larger, deeper, and richer each and every week?

Whether embodied in a word, catch phrase, play scenario, secret code, or entire world of metaphor, languages and worlds that therapists and their adolescent patients mutually create can become their own. These shared meanings become the powerful routes through which the teenager and therapist communicate best. They serve as shortcuts for teens between difficult life experiences and the voice that they give those experiences within the therapeutic context. Nowhere does the teenager and therapist feel more connected than in that unique space. Nowhere does the adolescent feel more understood and special.

12

FREE TO BE

Setting Limits in Therapy

We think of therapy as an all-inviting place where teenage patients come to let it all hang out, a space accepting of any and all forms of their self-expression. But, in reality, therapy doesn't quite work that way. If it did, teenage patients might choose to bring alcohol and drugs to enhance their hours or openness. They might bring friends to chill or have sex with. Some might take a leak out the window or pierce themselves in front of their therapist. Others would etch their names on the door and use permanent marker to cover the office walls with graffiti. For sure, many teenagers would stay longer than their 50 or so minutes, though others would be more inclined to leave early or burst in on another child's hour. Jealous patients would bully the next patient in line or scribble over artwork that other patients drew. When frustrated or confronted, they would break our windows and even strike out at us with their spit and fists or, more playfully, with open ketchup packets and "accidentally" spilled sodas. And we can only imagine what they'd choose to talk about. There's no end to the mischief and mayhem that adolescents might bring to their therapies. But, as we'll soon see, ruined clothing and vandalized walls would hardly be the worst of it.

PROTECT YOURSELF

Orlando was a seventh grader whose constant disruptions in class, utter refusal to do schoolwork, and frequent fighting was about to cost him his place at a respectable private school. The school's director, long frustrated by the boy's inability to benefit from his teachers' unfailing support, finally served an ultimatum when Orlando slammed a locker door on a boy's leg: He must get therapy and shape up or he'd be out of there.

> *When Orlando came to me, I met a 13-year-old who had little interest in treatment. "I don't need this," he said, "let him [the director] throw me out."*
>
> *"But don't you want to go to a good college some day?" his father asked.*
>
> *"I don't care if I go to school tomorrow," Orlando replied. His parents, who gave Orlando free rein at home, laughed, shrugged, and looked at me as if to say, "You do something."*
>
> *"Will you at least come to see Dr. Bromfield once or twice?" they asked.*
>
> *"What do I get if I come?"*
>
> *"We'll work that out," Orlando's parents said, turning to me. "He'll be here."*
>
> *As they walked out I could hear Orlando negotiate for a new video game today in exchange for his giving therapy a try tomorrow.*

Orlando did come and, to everyone's surprise, engaged quickly with me, needing no bribes to keep coming. He was an open child who readily warned me of his hot temper.

> *"You better watch what you say." Orlando pointed at me.*
>
> *"Or else?" I asked.*

"Let's just say you'd rather not know," he replied, wanting to sound tough, but seeming to mean it.

But Orlando's candid talk and his energetic bravado sometimes led me to forget his caution. "I wasn't kidding," he'd remind me with raised finger followed by minutes of the silent treatment. In time he reconnected and talked about ways that his anger had gotten him into trouble. He'd not shown any awareness of the profound narcissistic vulnerability that triggered his rage. Nor had he spoken a word of remorse for the times his angry actions or words had hurt people he cared for, such as his favorite teachers. That would change.

"She probably doesn't even care," Orlando said for the third time in one hour. Orlando referred to Mrs. Dunster, the skilled and devoted school counselor who routinely buoyed him and often patched the relationships and bridges he'd almost burned. Orlando had gotten into a pushing match in the gym just hours after Mrs. Dunster had once again defended him to the tiring director. Orlando had kicked the other boy.

"I had no choice," Orlando said. "Ketcher called me a fag. No one says that and gets away with it."

"And now you feel bad about it."

"I don't give a shit about Ketcher's leg!"

"I didn't mean Ketcher," I said. "I meant you feel bad about letting—"

"Watch it!" Orlando interrupted, picking up a wooden block.

"About letting Mrs. Dunster down," I continued, readying to duck just as Orlando whipped the large block. I dodged to the right and the block whizzed by my ear, smacking the door and denting it.

> *I rose to pick the block up and then sat back down. "You've got a choice to make, Orlando," I said calmly. Orlando stared at me, red with rage, panting. "You can stay and work."*
>
> *Orlando picked up a block. "Next time I won't miss."*
>
> *"Or leave." Orlando cocked his arm. "You throw that block and we're done with therapy."*
>
> *Orlando's chest heaved.*
>
> *"I'm serious. How can I possibly help you if I have to worry about catching a wooden block in my face."*
>
> *Orlando squeezed the block then whipped it hard but harmlessly at the doll house. "What does she care anyway? It's not like I'm her son or anything."*
>
> *"But somehow she cares about you, a lot, doesn't she?"*
>
> *"I know," Orlando said with tears. "Don't you think I fucking know that!"*

Orlando had done all the work he could do, up to a point. He and I kept bumping up against the wall of his sensitivity. He'd told me, he didn't want to switch to a new school for just the eighth grade, especially after having spent the past seven years in his present school. But he didn't have much time to gain understanding and self-control. As it happened, that session encouraged me to call the director and allude to a certain "breakthrough" in his therapy. "He cares and," I could honestly say, "I think he's heading upwards." This time Orlando didn't let anyone down. His therapy deepened, and he discovered the sources of his fragile esteem as well as his suppressed and strong wish to please the people he loved. Upon his graduation he received the most improved student award as he went off to secondary school.

I know, that makes it sound too easy. And what if, as can happen, he'd decided to throw the second block at me? Even if I'd set my limit while on the run, it was well-informed and nothing like a cavalier dare. Had Orlando felt my confrontation as something competitive or shaming, he'd probably have assaulted me or fled. I've seen many adolescent patients whom I'd never have challenged that way. My message here, however, is that my setting a limit on Orlando's aggression critically enabled his therapy to move on to new and necessary heights, or more aptly, depths. As therapists, we can only make our best guesses as to how and when to intervene.

How could I have done therapy if I had to fear that the words I had to say might lead to my getting smacked on the head? And what of my empathy? Could I have stayed as much on Orlando's side if he'd broken my glasses or my nose? My firmly putting Orlando's self-control back in his hands forced him to make a choice: give up or own his therapy. Although Orlando never again threw anything at me, he regularly vented his rage by throwing balls and objects into play settings that he'd engineered to be nondestructive. "That was your eyeball. I just fractured it in a million tiny pieces," he said, free of the greater guilt and self-hatred that really hurting me would have invoked, freer to explore his relationship with me and others.

How much aggression should therapists permit? I cannot imagine how letting a child beat me up, burn me, or tie me to a chair would help the child. What message would such passivity or masochism convey? I generally have no problem with a teenage patient playfully kicking my shoe, aiming a play gun at me, enacting a puppet devouring my hand, momentarily blocking my way to the door, or, as happens often, getting carried away while playing catch. I will heed the context and meaning of the aggression, and might even bring it up; I will not automatically, however, ask that it stop. In the end, when to set limits is a question best answered by a therapist's individual clinical taste, comfort, and judgment.

PROTECT PROPERTY

What can adolescent patients do with the therapists' office and things? I respond to that query with further questions. How will therapists feel if their patients slam their fists through the wall? That, for sure, is something a lot of teenagers feel like doing. Will we be able to maintain our sympathy and compassion for them, or will we suddenly see the same bad apple that parents and teachers have been griping about? And how will the teens deal with the consequences of their aggression? Limiting the intentional destruction of our offices and our things seems prudent. And yet, I can recall exceptions to that rule.

Leah was a bright, creative, and athletic 11-year-old who thoroughly hated her 8-year-old sister, Kristie. Leah regularly punched, scratched, and bit her younger sister. A crinkled nose was enough for Leah to attack. Leah wished aloud that Kristie would die or go away, and smiled a smile of true joy when she once described dreaming that it had come true. Leah's parents had brought their daughter to me with the justified fear that she'd one day hurt her sister badly. Where will it end, they worried.

> *"I hate her. I hate her ugly little face," Leah said while shredding the drawing she'd made of Kristie. "I think I'll make a model of Kristie and smash it." But Leah's frustration couldn't wait. Using her bare hands, she broke several craft sticks in half.*

"I can't stand this," she said, shaking her fists. "I want to kill her. That's the only thing that will make me feel better." Leah prowled the office in search of relief. She scanned the shelves, my desk, and finally ran her hand through a big wicker basket of puppets, stuffed animals, and dinosaurs. She took out baby doll.

For many minutes, Leah held the doll, saying nothing and looking stressed. Using her fingertips she gently felt the baby's neck then laughed. She rubbed the baby's neck until her hands formed a ring around the neck. Leah squeezed until her fingers turned white. I watched as Leah strangled the baby to death, its head suddenly falling off and dropping to the floor with a startling thud. Leah threw the baby to the basket and looked at me. "I'm sorry," she said in a panic. "I didn't mean to break it." Leah frantically tried to tape the head to the baby's body, but it kept coming off.

"You can't help it," I said calmly, holding the head and baby steady while she clumsily taped them together. "She's ruined your life." Leah nodded with all of the sadness a person of any age can feel.

Over time Leah broke other dolls and figures. I didn't mind. When a child is on the brink of genuine violence, *"Please,"* I think, *"break my toys."* How much better that she expressed her murderous rage in play than with a real sister. Likewise, I invite rather than censure destructive behavior from teens who are self-injurious. Rather than forbidding, I've welcomed: a suicidal teen carefully lining up miniature trucks and cars then flattening them with his heels (his father had a car collection he loved more than his children); an adolescent girl using scissors to slice up young children's books from my waiting room (she struggled to not cut herself); and, a bulimic girl's purposefully mushing a McDonald's hamburger into my carpet (her mother was controlling and obsessed with cleanliness). Each of these behaviors held meaning that hungered for safe expression. My accepting and appreciating the need behind these significant deeds has always inspired more trust and openness, enriched the therapy, and led to healthier, less self-hurting coping. In most cases, the behaviors have not gone on for long. I've also found that most adolescents on their own sooner or later make amends, though I have asked more conduct-disordered teenagers to replace what they'd intentionally broken.

CLEAN OR HAVE THEM CLEAN

To clean or not to clean is a distant cousin to the question of limits. Again, more than a simple rule is called for. The kinds of children I generally ask to pick up after themselves include teens lacking a reliable conscience, who lie, steal, and cheat their way through life; teens whose modus operandi is to create messes for others to clean; teens who are clearly testing me (e.g., who eye me while tossing crumpled sheets of paper on the floor); teens who unthinkingly litter the office with candy wrappers or who rest their muddied boots on my walls. After a wrenching hour, I might also ask an adolescent to clean up to give them an unemotional few moments to regroup before walking back into the world.

Who do I not ask to clean? Teens who do nothing but please and meet other people's needs, such as those with narcissistically preoccupied parents; teens who already work too hard in their lives; teens who are too inhibited or who never protest or assert themselves; and, teens for whom control is a major life issue. It may seem contradictory, but I tend not to ask bossy adolescents to pick up after themselves. Therapists' arbitrarily creating control struggles can offer little, as it did with Stan, a sixth grader who avoided every reasonable demand for a child his age.

Twelve-year-old Stan picked up, inspected, and dropped most everything in the office. He stepped here and there to avoid tripping on the things he'd left everywhere. Our time was about up and he, ignoring my request to help clean, watched me do it.

"You really want me to clean?" he asked when I was halfway done.

"Your call," I replied. Stan surveyed the room. "You're doing a pretty good job by yourself. I think I'll leave it to you." I nodded my okay with that. The next week Stan cleaned up wholly by himself without my asking him to lift a finger.

A controlling and guilt-inducing therapist was the last thing Stan needed while contending with his severe control issues and a stunted quest for self-autonomy.

Adolescent patients tend to test all limits, including those related to the time frame of therapy. They may offer to clean up, only after their time has run out and they are now meeting on their therapist's dime: "Thanks for offering, but I have to get on with my schedule." Such a remark confirms the considerate aspect of the teenager's gesture while highlighting other possible motives.

Keep in mind, too, that while limits can help adolescent patients find more freedom in therapy, they also can hamper it. I never limit what teenagers' say in their hours. If profane, dark, hostile, sexual, sadistic, frightening, and suicidal talk doesn't belong in therapy, where does it belong? Nor do I demand that teens talk in politically correct terms. That, however, doesn't mean I don't notice what teens say and call therapeutic attention to it. Therapists don't drink and smoke or get physically cozy with their patients; though—isn't there always a but?—I once indulged a marijuana-addicted teenager's request to come to his session stoned. He wanted me to tell him whether he was as enlightened and insightful when high as he imagined himself to be. (I had to tell him that he was duller and more detached.) I've watched a cutting adolescent hurt herself, a test and ritual that I needed to both pass and witness in order to win the trust that led to her recovery. And I refrain from pushing adolescents into a corner, physically or emotionally. Most of all, it will be the therapist's dependable expectations and ways, fair attitudes, and steady maintenance of the therapy's framework that will convince his adolescent patients that he is serious about helping them find their a way out of their hurts and difficulties.

13

ALL THAT JAZZ

Educating, Problem-Solving, Advocating:
Helping Teens Beyond Formal Therapy

When I began doing psychotherapy with teenagers and children, I was naïve, I saw myself as a purist. I didn't have a large Oriental rug bounded by figurines or an analytic couch, but I believed that I could get it all done by just listening and dropping an occasional pearl of interpretive wisdom. I imagined that children would need nothing more than the puppets, the doll house, and their words to express their inner conflicts, and this, in turn, would free them from anxieties, depressions, phobias, and the like. However, hard realities whacked me on the head. No children I saw seemed able to analyze their way out of Crohn's disease, a real learning disability, or an abusive history. Nor did simple play and talk seem to be enough for children facing fears or coping with trauma. As happens with much in therapy, I found my young patients teaching me that I needed to find other means of helping them. And so, hour by hour, I gradually added therapeutic tools to my repertoire, picking up ideas, skills, and exercises that helped me to help adolescents take healthier charge of their lives.

PROBLEM-SOLVE

I first applied the term *problem solve* to my work in therapy
when learning how to persuade insurance companies to pay for
my patients' treatments. I'd first tried putting "Psychoanalytic
Psychotherapy" on the forms, but payments were denied; "psy-
chodynamic" and "relationship-based" did no better. Finally,
with what I then thought was a stroke of reframing genius, I
described the treatment modality as *problem-solving therapy*.
Little did I know what my future in therapy would bring and
how accurate I was being.

> *"No comment." Eleven-year-old X-Man, as he liked to be
> called, sat straight up on the edge of the big chair, his legs
> swinging back and forth against the seat. Though I'd assumed
> he'd heard that remark on television, there was no irony or
> humor in his words. He focused intensely on a hand-held
> video game.*

X-Man's mother had called me the previous week. She
told me that Xavier was regressing in school and at home,
that he was refusing to go to physical therapy, and wouldn't
wear his leg braces. She said he was arguing with his beloved
aide and a couple of times he just lay down in the school hall-
way, requiring two teachers to carry him to a wheelchair. "I
haven't seen him like this for a long time," Xavier's mother
said.

It'd been almost a year since I'd finished up with Xavier, a
boy with cerebral palsy. He'd come to me because of babyish
behaviors at home and school and a growing lack of compliance
with his small army of support people, including physical, occupational, and speech therapists. He'd sit down and cry when

facing the 15 feet of ramp that led from his classroom to the cafeteria, and he wouldn't try to read or do any homework. All he wanted was to play video games.

"What's up, X-Man?" I asked. "I haven't seen you for awhile."
"Let's just keep it that way," he replied.

X-Man and I had enjoyed a tight working relationship. He'd held our meetings and his therapy in the highest regard. I'd been his confidante, the one he'd bring his complaints and annoyances to. And he'd made startling progress. Xavier had become the star pupil, cooperative and daring, and proud of his accomplishments. He'd taken to skiing, and with enthusiasm and shaky legs would brave the cold, ski lift, and slopes. He'd even grown accustomed to wearing his orthotic braces. "Everyone can see how much I've grown up!" he'd announced in the last meeting we'd had before terminating.

I knew X-man well enough to know that his obsessing on a video game, the stiff posture, the sarcasm, and silence all signaled one thing.
"Xavier," I began, "something's bugging you—a lot!"
X-Man burst into tears. "I hate, I can't stand, I don't know," a jumble of words all came out at once garbled by sobbing.

When the tears passed, X-Man and I talked. He told me how he hated the hospital. He'd had two heart surgeries and had flown to the Midwest to have a third operation, an extremely specialized surgery on his leg nerves to help reduce the spasticity of his leg muscles. When X-Man screamed about hospi-

tals, doctors, needles, casts, and bad-tasting medicines, he knew
what he was talking about. He spoke, too, with sadness, about
having cerebral palsy, how it had ruined his life, taken away
all his fun, and doomed him to be different and weird. At last,
he shared the precipitant to his current agony.

> *"I can't take it," he said. "I can't wait. It's scaring me too
> much. I just want to get it over."*
> *"Get what over?" I asked gently.*
> *"Get my mother," he replied. "She'll explain it to you."*

His mother told me that Xavier was scheduled for another
major surgery in the summer, 10 months from then. The pro-
cedure would deliberately break then reassemble his hips. The
recovery period would be long and hard, with X-Man having to
wear a lower body cast for many weeks.

> *"What can I do to help?" I asked Xavier.*
> *"I'm afraid I'll die when they make me sleep," he cried.
> "Get it over, I can't take waiting."*
> *"You'd like me to call the surgeon and see if he can do it
> sooner?" I asked.*
> *"Yes, please!" he yelled, wanting it done yesterday.*

Once Xavier had identified the issue, we were able to do some
good problem solving. I'd call the surgeon (who agreed to operate many months early). We also together devised some strategies to help him cope with the wait. Whenever he felt the scary
feeling coming over him, he'd go tell his mother about his being
afraid of never waking up. If that wasn't enough, he could call me
(he never had to). Before he got frantic, he'd remind himself
about how nice the nurses were to him at the hospital (he did this

frequently). Rather than worry about the surgery every waking minute, Xavier agreed to defer his fears for a 15-minute period after dinner reserved for nothing but worry about the operation (many nights he got bored after the first few minutes). He also suggested getting a new hand-held video game system the day after his surgery, as a distraction to look forward to now and something to help manage the boredom of his rehabilitation, an idea his mother and I thought was excellent.

It had taken the comfort of our solid relationship and some traditional talk to get to the immediate obstruction. But right then and there, our mutual and more active problem solving helped establish an action plan that transformed 10 months of regression and anguish into a relatively bearable month of waiting. Xavier has since thanked me many times for helping to get him through this major ordeal.

Problem solving in therapy can deal with almost any problem, big or little, present or future. *"How are we going to get you through finals given your anger at the school?"; "How are you going to stay in control tomorrow when that kid calls you a pussy again?"; "What can you do to get your dad to understand?"; "What,* we ask together, *will happen if you do that?"*

EDUCATE

Hardly a day goes by that I don't educate some teen about something. In response to their direct questions, I'll explain what AIDS is or what the Vietnam War was about. I'll help them to understand the difference between the flu and a bacterial infection or explain to them how college and graduate school work. I may take them aside—meaning, calling a time out in their therapy proper—to correct some misconception, explaining in clinical

terms why I know that they do not have schizophrenia or clarifying why their view of what safe sex means is naïve and mistaken.

> *"I can't wait until I get home. I'm going to go on IM and tell
> everyone that she's a fucking ho and that she gave us all blow
> jobs in the gym."*

Anyone who knows teens won't find this paragraph shocking
or out of the ordinary. A girl had cruelly rejected Charlie in
front of other kids and he was hurt. I understood his wish for
revenge by humiliating her as she had done to him. Yet, I also
knew that doing so could put him at risk. I explained to Charlie that what he wrote might become something of a public
document. I told him of instances where teenagers I'd known
got arrested or put on social probation for mouthing off online.

> *"But she treated me like dirt. I never did that to her,"* he came
> back.
> *"It'll look like harassment,"* I said, *"and no one will want
> to hear your sob story."*

My information sobered Charlie's fantasy, but he was appre-
ciative. The last thing he wanted to give that girl was the
chance to undo his solid high school record. "She could ruin
my whole life," he decided. My educating Charlie, my providing him with information to enhance his decision making, was
not an exception; it happens all the time with adolescents.

ADVOCATE

I've found that one of the hardest things for young therapists
to grasp is how central they are to an adolescent's life. You, I

tell them, may be the only person in the world who understands her plight, sees the complications of her home, understands her strengths and weaknesses, recognizes the school-related issues, and knows the likely path to redemption and growth. The therapist's is often the clearest vision in an ocean of confusion and competing alliances.

Sean was an adopted 17-year-old who, referred on the orders of the court, had been making progress in therapy. He'd stopped stealing, lied less often, he'd grown dependable about coming to sessions, and was open and honest during his hours. His parents reported that he had begun helping out at home by stacking firewood and painting the shed. Though he owed his parents much money, he'd found a job, and was paying his parents back on a weekly basis. Most convincing of all, he was dropping his gangster persona and showing more vulnerability and sadness. He was losing bad friends and trying to find better ones. But life has a way of throwing wrenches into the works. A bad decision led to his being in the wrong place at the right time, or at least, at the time that the local police burst in.

Sean was at risk of going to prison for six months. What would he learn there, I pondered. A stint in a teen drug group had only taught him to use more drugs than the weed smoking that had led to his being there. Jail will toughen and teach him to be more criminal, that's what I expected. And so, holding onto his more recent growth, and judging jail to be a destructive force on his horizon, I appealed to the district judge he came before. The judge, who knew my work and that Sean's therapy was rather new, extended his probation and gave him another six months to show that he could be more mature and law-abiding. Thankful for the extra chance, Sean continued his work in therapy. Though there were future ups and downs, Sean mostly ramped upward, ultimately returning to community college, finding full-time employment, and becoming a decent citizen.

Of course, it doesn't always work so well. Many times I have advocated—stuck my neck out, given my word, begged that a teen be given one more chance—only to have been burnt by the adolescent.

COACH

By coaching I mean getting involved in ways that give teenage patients guidance and encouragement in their lives outside of treatment. I find myself coaching most with three types of adolescents: those who are somewhat stuck and lack the confidence to take risks, and need a gentle push; those who are on the fence between moral and delinquent behavior; and, those who lack reliable and able parents. Not so rarely, a teen fits all three categories. Consider Angelica, a socially anxious 18-year-old who barely graduated from high school. A career in marketing was all she'd ever wanted, but she had neither hope nor any idea for getting there.

In our work together, alongside my listening to her talking of insecurities and fears, I'd regularly give Angelica tangible assistance in targeting a marketing job. She worked on her junior college application during her hour, and once accepted, we together read the catalogue of courses. I showed her how to use a newspaper's classified web page to find advertised jobs, and gently nudged her not to run away from two job interviews. Angelica soon found a job as an assistant manager at a chain discount department store. She then used therapy to help figure out dilemmas with customers, bosses, and fellow employees. Part-time cheerleader, career counselor, mediator, computer consultant, and personal editor, I did whatever I could to support Angelica's pursuit of the life she wanted. Meanwhile, Angelica continued to spend much of her therapy hours talking about feelings, including what it had been like to grow up with no adult guidance. She clearly saw my help as a transitional step toward standing more on her own and trusting her own judgment and abilities. I've likewise coached teens in ways they might organize themselves academically, prepare for college admissions, and start their own businesses.

Coaching also includes my teaching or exposing teenagers to strategies and resources that might facilitate their reaching the goals of therapy. I demonstrate behavioral strategies that can relieve their symptoms or foster more adaptive behaviors. I teach stressed teens how to meditate and systematically stretch. I show adolescents who get headaches and stomachaches how to use visual imagery to relax as well as to safely express inwardly targeted frustration and anger. I've prescribed low-grade aerobic exercise to teens with chronic fatigue and urged more intense workouts for those distressed by overly high levels of energy and tension. I advise young insomniacs on how to get to sleep and how to stay there. I give them suggestions about their study habits and help them to find study guides and tutors. And, as you might guess, I try to help teens who rely on alcohol or drugs for self-medication to find their own ways of quelling and soothing their agitation and unease. Oftentimes, I help most by referring teenagers to other practitioners or agencies, that have ancillary benefits to offer. There's no end to the ways that therapists help their adolescent patients. I'd bet that many readers could generate lists far longer and more creative than my own.

14

THINKING OUTSIDE THE COUCH

Getting Therapeutically Creative

Seasoned elementary schoolteachers live by this credo: Start the year firm, with clear expectations, plenty of structure, high standards, and ample consequences. Only after the year progresses and students have learned to live according to the rules of their classroom, do these teachers loosen up. We could do worse as therapists than to follow this example. Begin each therapy with a framework—when we meet, for how long, where, and how we talk and what we do—that is sturdy and certain enough. It can be altered later and only when clinically indicated. By *indicated* I mean a clinical situation where doing things a tad or a lot out of the ordinary may offer more benefit than it costs, may bring more therapeutic clarity than confusion, and may advance the therapy in ways that might not otherwise happen as quickly or at all. Constructive creativity can enhance almost any human endeavor. Why would it differ for the therapist?

COMMUNICATE OUTSIDE THE HOUR

In over two decades of doing therapy I've invited a majority of my teenage patients to use my telephone number. I could count on one hand the number of times in a year that they call. On the other hand, many of my adolescent patients have taken to e-mailing me. Why would I encourage this (I give new patients my card with my Internet address), and what is it about e-mail that works for them?

Martin was a teenager who'd been diagnosed with severe learning disabilities, attention deficit, and oppositional disorder. The director of the learning clinic at one of Boston's most prominent hospitals had described him as the most dyslexic child she'd ever met. She had no qualms about predicting he'd never make it through high school. She warned his parents that he'd never become a self-sufficient student or adult and encouraged them to prepare—educationally, financially, and emotionally—for that certainty.

> *To: RichardBromfield@telicom.com*
> *Subject: Help!!!!!!!!!!*
> *Dear RB:*
>   *I can't take it anymor. The stres is kiling me. I got an englisj compisishin do tomorrow and a math thing and my mothe's on my cas cos I was suposd to help my neybor and I'm gona kil sumone if I don't get help!!!!!!! your rite what you said was rite. I do put to much preshor on me to much. Why can't I jus be happy with doing okay lik evryone els.? Thnkas, Martin You don't hav to rite back but Im reddy to kil sumone.*

Once Martin discovered e-mail, he took to e-mailing me daily, sometimes more than once. For a long time his messages spoke of his enormous frustration coping with the demands of a mostly mainstreamed public education. He'd report on the school demands of the day, his perennial fear that he'd never make it through them, and his anger that his (loving and supportive) parents somehow were never helping him enough. In my responses I'd strive to make clear that his plight had been heard and confirm the value of his efforts.

> *Dear Martin,*
>
> *Thanks for the e-mail. That English paper sounds hard. I wonder if it as hard as the one you did last month and got a B on? I know what you mean, too. Mothers worry about things like helping neighbors, don't they? I hope you don't have to kill anyone. See you Thursday.*
>
> *RB*

Martin would generally mail me back with appreciation and news of his having made it through yesterday's ordeal with success. He'd then go on to complain about a new and tougher challenge bearing down on him that day. As I watched him from a distance, I knew that he'd be able to handle it, and yet, I also could see how frightened he was and how little yesterday's success buoyed him for tomorrow. Our messaging served as a constant testimony to what he'd done and how he could do even better the next time.

> *Dear RB:*
>
> *I volunteered to help run the school fair next wek. I must be crazie. I cant even do what I hav to for school alreddy. But I thot it wood look good on my job record for colleg and stuff. If I go crazie wil you help me and wil you remind me not to never agin be stupid enuf to ask to run a school fair. Thanks, Martin*

Over time Martin's therapy and e-mails dealt with his wish to accomplish and be special. Though the psychologist who'd tested him had talked of self-contained special education schools, Martin was thriving in a public school with the assistance of special education. His parents had gone to graduate school and his siblings had graduated from selective colleges, but none of them had been as hungry to learn and succeed as Martin. And none of them had worked any harder. Our e-mailing provided ongoing support as Martin pursued harder and bigger goals.

> *Dear Martin:*
> *How exciting. The school fair is important. Didn't you say it raised money for charity, like that shelter for battered women? Your helping is something to be proud of. RB PS If doing something good for your community is crazy, then I wish more people were crazy.*

Needless to say, these samplings can barely tell about a therapy that extended for years and involved thousands of e-mails covering a wide range of life experiences and developmental phases. Over time Martin's e-mails sharpened in their focus, and their spelling and grammar improved dramatically (he learned to use a spelling checker). Martin's life continued to advance just as well. He made National Honor Society and was an active participant in many school activities. He became a good driver, a talented camp counselor, and a wonderful speaker. An op-ed that he wrote on special education was published in Boston's major newspaper and he was accepted with a merit scholarship to the college of his choice.

> *Dear RB:*
> *Sorry I didn't write for awhile. I had two exams and it's making me pretty ankshis. But I am proud too. I got an A on*

my accounting quiz and B+ on my English essay. Patty's help (my tutor) helped me a ton. Sorry I haven't been writing. I've been trying to see if I can do okay on my own. And I think I am doing okay. Someone wants me to study with them. Got to go. Martin

Although there were many reasons why e-mail facilitated Martin's work with me, the bottom-line was that it gave Martin more of me and therapy every day. And why wouldn't he want that? When you think of it, an hour or so isn't a whole lot of time to process a week's worth of experience, no less the childhood that came before. We are apt to forget this when seeing teens who keep asking us what time it is. But, for all of its value, some therapists might reasonably wonder why I'd encourage patients to e-mail. Don't we have more than enough to do already? Of course, the answer has to be, yes, we do. Yet, my reasons for e-mailing are not as altruistic as one might guess.

E-mailing can help to better understand what's going on with my patients; promote their bonding with me; offer a more direct window to the facts of their lives, information that often doesn't come out in the therapy hour; and, nurture their growing commitment to treatment. It allows me to continue working with these teenagers in between hours and provides me with the opportunity to finish incomplete discussions, clarify misunderstandings, and influence my young patients' behavior and decision making when they are away from therapy. Some teenagers (and adults) are able to convey through e-mail material what they feel too ashamed or uncomfortable to say in person. And though most of my patients seldom, if ever, e-mail me, my simple offer to read their e-mail has touched reluctant teens, persuading them to give me and therapy a chance. At its essence, this extratherapy form of communication helps me do therapy better; and doing therapy better helps me avoid crises, stress, and burnout.

SHOW ME

One picture can be worth a lot of words. More critically, it can allow therapists to see what an adolescent is trying to tell them. Finally, it can open or widen an avenue to explore, as it did for one 12-year-old girl brought to me because of near-crippling jealousy for her younger brother, jealousy that she could neither admit nor manage.

> *"I don't know how to explain it. "All I know is that he does it and I can't stand him." Jennifer clenched her fists.*

Jennifer had been trying to describe how her 9-year-old brother's night prowling ruined her sleep every night. I'd asked her to explain what about his night behavior had bothered her so much, but she couldn't find the words.

> *"Might showing me what your house looks like help?" I asked. I walked to the desk and put a piece of paper down. Jennifer, anxious to escape her frustration, moved to the desk. She studied the paper for some time, then drew a large rectangle divided by various shaped squares and smaller rectangles.*
> *"This," she said, pointing to one square, "is my room. This is my bureau, this is my desk, and this is my bed." Jennifer scribbled some cute and fuzzy little animals. "That," she went on with giggles, "is my cat, Coconut. She sleeps on my head. And those are my favorite stuffed monkey and kangaroo." She laughed. "They're older than I am." Jennifer started to draw again, then suddenly stopped, lost in thought. "Wow! David wasn't even alive yet."*
> *Jennifer went on to draw her parents' and David's bedroom. "See," he creeps out of here, real sneaky like, and then*

when he gets here," she fingered her parents' bedroom, "he climbs in on my father's side. I always hear my mother and father say, 'Go back to bed, David.'" Jennifer mocked what she heard as her parents' weak tone. "'You have to sleep in your own bed.'" Jennifer put the pencil down and looked at me, her frustration grew. "'You're way too old to be sleeping in our bed,' Then I hear him whine, and they say, 'No, David!'" Jennifer was pissed. "Then I hear him climb in their bed and I hear him laughing and talking to my parents." With tears in her eyes Jennifer used all her strength to break the short pencil in half. "I hate him! He ruined everything!"

I often ask teenagers to draw me their homes, rooms, or the cars where they experienced family strife. "Use these to build the classroom," I said recently, handing wooden blocks and Playmobil figures to a junior high school student suffering excruciating panic and fainting at school. That teenager gladly built her class, showing me with hard objects how the crowded room made her feel trapped and stuck too close to other students. I find teens are ever open to using toys to reenact situations too hard, complex, or tedious to explain with mere words.

"Show me!" I routinely urge adolescents. "Show me the rap you sang that led to the fight." "Show me the face you made that you can't believe got you a detention." And, just for the record, know that my use of *Show me* is not restricted to bad stuff. "Go ahead," I urge my young patients when they speak of Karaoke routines, 100 push-ups, or mean juggling that they wish I could see for myself. What's unreasonable about an adolescent wanting a trusted grown-up to admire and think well of them?

HELP TEENS EXPRESS THEMSELVES

Some time ago I treated Alfonse, a 16-year-old who'd tried to kill himself by taking a bottle of Tylenol. Upon his discharge from the hospital, we began meeting twice a week. For the first several weeks, he barely spoke to me. When I asked him how he saw himself, he drew a picture of a stinking heap of shit. When I asked what he saw for his future, he drew himself, dead, hanging by his neck from a tree. I asked more, but he said he didn't like drawing. How about a rap song? I said, somewhat flippantly, not sure where to go next. To my surprise and intrigue, Alfonse took a notebook from my desk and started writing.

> *He tells me to write a song,*
> *No way I'm going to make it long,*
> *I don't know why he asks but I don't mind it,*
> *Even though they are shit,*
> *Sometimes it gets on my nerves,*
> *When he asks me questions about fags and perves,*
> *Other than that I don't have any cares,*
> *Unless he just sits and he just stares.*

Alfonse handed me the notebook and after I'd read it, asked me to remind him of all the questions I'd asked but he hadn't answered in previous sessions. He wrote his replies quickly and with satisfaction, as when I again asked how school goes.

> *He's so lazy,*
> *He's so lazy it's crazy,*
> *He sits on his ass,*
> *Every now and then passes gas,*

He's a slob,
A big fat slob,
He watches TV and keeps to himself,
Doesn't even read the books on his shelf,
How can he live this way,
It makes me wonder if he is gay.

For all of their simplicity, Alfonse's rap suggested many levels of experience: self-awareness, self-hatred, some realistic self-perception, fears of being homosexual, and hints of something sexual having occurred when he was an 8-year-old boy. Alfonse continued writing these impromptu poems for many weeks until, one session, he decided it'd just be easier to talk.

I've encouraged some teen patients to keep journals, and many have done so readily. Writing to oneself can bring comfort and awareness, and serve as a repository for thoughts, feelings, and experiences that occur between therapy meetings. Some patients have chosen to use their journals as starting points for each hour, a resource that helped them cope with the demands of therapy. In between meetings, their journals functioned as a substitute for me, someone who'd listen to and care deeply about what they lived and wrote about.

But, such self-expressions do not have to be limited to the artistically inclined or talented. After all, most adolescents do not want to keep journals or write poems for their therapists. Yet, most of them will happily share with us their favorite songs, movies, books, and even comic books. "How is your room decorated?" I've asked. "Tell me how you pick out your clothes?" "If you could have a car, what would it look like?" Such questions, and the objects of their focus, can reveal much about how teenagers see and would like to see themselves.

DISCLOSE

At certain times in their therapies, my teenage patients take great interest in my earlier life. *"Did you ever screw up?"* they ask. *"Do you know what it's like to feel like a complete waste?"* *"Did you ever embarrass yourself with a girl you liked?"* At particularly opportune moments, I've shared experiences, such as my not getting serious about school until my junior year, my loving hockey but not being good enough to play on the varsity team, and my growing up in a working-class neighborhood. Hearing that I am fallible and have known difficult, shaming, and ugly moments, and that I have survived and, in their eyes, thrived, has buoyed my teenage patients against their own despair and self-doubt.

I find disclosing to be a tricky enterprise, however. I'm often most moved to share something personal with a teenage whom I like and wish to comfort or connect with. And occasionally, I've disclosed something that seemed modest and yet it appeared to burden the child. How do we assess the wisdom of our revealing some piece of background or experience about ourselves? Am I sharing this, I wonder, for myself or to promote clinical movement that will otherwise be lost? Is this for me or them? Coming to a neat decision can be harder than it sounds, and when I'm unsure, I err on the conservative side and do not disclose.

STRETCH TO NEW PLACES

Being creative as a therapist can sound like too much work; often, it refers to our just being flexible and adapting to teenage patients and their needs. Consider this list of accommodations I've made for patients:

- Within reason I'll try to reschedule, for example, to meet an adolescent's wish to go to a concert or meet friends.
- I'll occasionally bring in a book or piece of music that I suspect will somehow touch or enrich a child's treatment.
- I spent several meetings helping a teenage retarded girl learn to properly shake hands, and for her to reconceptualize a firm shake as the kind of affectionate hug she ever (inappropriately) gave and demanded from others.
- With some trepidation I've suggested parents buy their socially isolated children more with-it clothes and haircuts.
- I keep Band-Aids on hand and eagerly fetch water for the thirsty, food for the starved, and ice bags for the wounded. I keep a throw on the chair for the chilly and open the window for someone who's "dying of the heat."
- Even though I do traditional talking relationship-based psychotherapy, I'll happily teach anxious and stressed teens how to meditate, stretch, and visualize relaxing imagery. Just as I'll help obese teens make sense of diets and exercise.
- When an adolescent's request to see my dog holds meaning and merit, I'll indulge it.

Of course, stretching ourselves, altering the framework, and getting creative can go too far, and in themselves do not guarantee therapeutic benefit. Therapists' improvisations are warranted only in the sense that they respect and follow the overriding structure, tenor, pace, and moment-by-moment needs of any one therapy with any one child.

15

YAWN

Moving Beyond Boredom and the Doldrums

Every course of therapy hits a wall now and then. It can be short-lived, one of many stops and starts up a long, steady road, or prolonged, as in a therapy that's rocky throughout. In the worst cases, the impasse can become permanent, wholly obstructing progress and leading to the adolescent's premature termination. What accounts for the therapeutic doldrums and what can therapists do to counter their gravity?

PROBE BOREDOM

Prick hate, and you are likely to find love or some derivative underneath. Fear, rage, resentment, and jealousy scream to be noticed. Emotions are by nature palpable and vital. Boredom, on the other hand, is like a black hole that can suck the life out of anything; it can slow the most robust therapy to a quietly grinding halt. Or it can take the form of a leaden albatross the therapy ever drags along. For all of its seeming nothingness, boredom can be a relevant, profound, and meaningful force in a teenager's therapy and life.

*Paul, a tall, athletic tenth grader, played with his sneaker lace
and looked at the clock. "We stop at 10 to 2, right?" he asked.*

*"Two on the nose," I replied. Paul sighed and fell back in
his chair. "Fifty minutes can seem like a long time," I added.*

*Paul looked at the clock again. Not a minute had passed.
We smiled and he returned to his sneaker lace.*

Less than four months before, Paul's therapy had gotten off
to a fast start. In his first hours he'd talked nonstop and in detail about barely passing grades despite gifted intelligence;
mediocre track meet times though athletically talented; horrid
friction with his mother; and, what bothered him most of all,
a lack of passion in his life. "Life bores me," he said. "But it
shouldn't. I'm too laid back." Paul complained of his previous
therapist, "All he did was ask yes or no questions that went
nowhere." Paul even cried with me. "That's never happened,"
he'd said, leaving our meeting enlivened and hopeful.

Paul's therapy continued to thrive for some time. He pulled
his failing grades up to Cs. He was examining his conflict with
his mother and was questioning what lay under his avoidance
of schoolwork and his estrangement from peers. "I think therapy is clicking," he said, even though he was beginning to talk
less, required more prodding, showed less affect, and watched
the time. Over several weeks, his momentum faded steadily
as if a wagon rolling up a long, slow incline.

*"You know." Paul sat up and shook himself alert. "I'm just
going to start talking. I'm just going to say whatever comes
into my head. That's got to be better than nothing, right?"*

"You'd think so," I agreed.

*Paul looked at me and opened his mouth. Nothing came out.
He looked to the ceiling, trying to think of something, then to the
clock. At the hour's end he looked at me apologetically and left.*

I was lost. My remarks—open-ended, provocative, or confirming—fell impotently by the wayside. I let pauses linger in the hope that some feeling might explode onto the scene. I didn't want to turn into his earlier, disliked therapist, the one who asked too many useless questions. Nonetheless, I was asking less helpful questions more frequently. The ticking of the clock was the only sound. It was only in the smallest recess of the office that our way back to connection would be found.

Paul burst into the next hour with forced enthusiasm and an obligatory proclamation that he was really going to talk this time. What felt to be hours later, we still sat in silence. Fifteen minutes to go. Paul no longer tried to speak. He stared. I no longer asked, "What is it?" "What are you thinking?" That only made him feel worse and pushed him farther inward. Mostly to amuse myself, I studied his stare. I noticed an unusual pattern. He stared at the right corner of the room for several minutes, then switched to the other side, then to the upper left corner, then to the upper right.

I looked to where Paul gazed and stared there myself. He didn't notice. Whenever he moved his eyes, I followed. "Paul," I said, startling him.

"Huh?"

I looked to one corner of the room and held my gaze until I'd actually forgotten Paul was there. I looked up. He watched me closely. I fell into a second stare, then a third and a fourth. When I came to, I saw that we'd gone over our time.

"You noticed," Paul said.

"I think I might have," I replied.

Paul walked out looking some combination of surprised, embarrassed, and intrigued.

As we'll see later in this chapter, boredom can be empty, but in Paul's case it was chock full.

> *Paul came to his next hour early. "You knew," he said on the*
> *way in and with a genuine liveliness that I hadn't seen before.*
> *"How?"*
> *"I watched."*
> *We smiled.*

Paul talked more about his staring. It was a compulsion that went back years, one that had begun with his simple staring at a spot in the immediate landscape, like a dust ball on a carpet, or in our case, a fleur-de-lis on my wallpaper. This way of staring had gradually evolved to a more complex behavior in which he'd imagine concentric circles surrounding the spot, circles that grew wavy and flowed inward, like ocean tides. He didn't know where this idea had come from, though, he said, he'd always liked the beach and had found watching the movement of the ocean soothing. He'd stare in one direction, he further explained, until the asymmetry distressed him and drove his stare to the point exactly opposite to where he'd been looking. He'd repeat ad infinitum until the arc of his staring had created a lovely, two-dimensional curve of focus resembling a satellite dish. Putting his strange, idiosyncratic, complicated, and near unconscious habit into words that I could understand was no mean feat. The shame he felt over this behavior had only made his revelation harder.

We also learned that the all-important precipitant to Paul's visual compulsion and what it served to distract him from was a frightening impulse to kill himself. He described the relentless pain of forever letting down his parents, teachers, and coaches. He felt harsh guilt over the natural talents that he squandered, especially when he could see people with much less working much harder than he did, achieving more, and being so much more thankful for what they had.

Bringing his compulsion to light made Paul need it less and freed him to explore other matters. He saw how his fear of commitment and closeness blocked his engaging with school, sports, friends, and himself. "I think I was more overwhelmed than bored," Paul said some weeks later. His discovery has since cautioned me not to take a teen patient's boredom at face value.

COMPREHEND AND DISARM RESISTANCE

We often think of patients as being resistant to therapy and even to us, their therapists. Resistance, however, aims more at feelings, thoughts, realities, and change that patients wish or need to fend off. We must watch out not to take resistance personally—though, as I'll show later, it can be—while enabling our young patients to use us in ways that catalyze their therapy. We try to move to the side just enough to stay out of the way, ever trying to help these teenagers own their conflicts and issues.

Neil was a remarkably hard worker. But when he got paid, his money would burn a hole in his pocket. He had an intellectual grasp of the value of saving, and yet, not buying what he wanted frustrated him too much. Over the previous year, he'd emptied his bank account and borrowed several hundreds dollars from his parents.

> "You're pissed off that I spent the $450 I made this summer on a stupid remote control car. I can tell you're pissed."
> "How can you tell?" I asked.
> "How could you not be? It was a stupid thing to do." I waited. "Shit, I wish I had that money. The car sucks, too."

Through moments such as these, Neil gained awareness that he was the one who disliked the way he managed his money. Soon enough he learned to protect his hard-earned wages from his more impulsively spending himself.

Resistance can manifest itself in an endless variety of ways. Consider the following examples: Toni was an 11-year-old girl with Asperger's syndrome who'd get into fights with other children when they wouldn't follow the rigid rules she set on the playground.

> *"I know it's hard to hear, Toni, but your fights are getting in the way of friends."*
> *Toni hummed.*
> *"You want everyone to do things just the way you want them to, and when they don't . . ."*
> *And hummed.*
> *"You get angry."*
> *Her humming grew louder.*

I'd talk and Toni hummed.

> *"Do you think I like having no friends?" she finally blared.*
> *"Not at all," I said softly.*
> *Toni hummed.*
> *"You want friends but aren't sure how to make them."*

Toni worked on this at a snail's pace, wanting not to hear what I said but wanting more to be less lonely. As her defensiveness lessened, she grew more open to discussing her social awkwardness and steps she could take to improve it.

Sela was an immature ninth grader. She refused to do schoolwork and would not do any chores at home. Yet she constantly pushed her parents to buy her video games and equipment. She'd demand monetary rewards for simple acts like riding the school bus and putting away the milk. She even insisted she deserved to be paid for coming to therapy.

> *"You are furious with me," I said.*
> *"What?" Sela asked as she struggled to open her eyes.*
> *"You're furious at me for urging your parents not to pay you for coming here."*
> *"I'm furious about what?" she asked, again opening her eyes.*
> *I started to explain but could see that she was asleep. She slept through the rest of that hour.*

Sela was indeed enraged, but not at me. My acceptance of her need to resist what I said, through genuine sleep, helped her to confront what she'd really felt. She was angry at herself that she'd become such a "pathetic and controlling and selfish child." She slept, she said, because she hated thinking that I could feel that way about her, too. I'll confess. I felt odd when her parents asked me if what she said was true, that she sleeps in therapy—teens like to provoke their parents that way; and yet, what choice did I have? I had to let her do it, and I had to admit that I did.

> *"I think I'm going to stop coming," Wes said. "I don't think I need it anymore. Things are going pretty well now."*

Wes's life was a train wreck, to use a cliché. He'd only been in therapy for five sessions and nothing had changed. If anything, his life was more complicated in a bad way than it had been when we met.

"I really appreciate how you've helped me. I understand my-self much better now. I think I can do it on my own now."

Wes was facing a probation hearing, three failing grades, and a lot else that wasn't good,

I asked my parents and they said it was up to you. So, you'll tell my parents that we're all set. Today will be my last day, right?"

The news didn't throw me. Wes's parents abdicated most of their parental duties. They'd brought him to me only because their attorney said it would be a wise move before Wes appeared in court.

"You know, Wes," I finally spoke. "I know it's too much to think about all the stuff you are up against. You probably can't imagine anything good happening in your life again. But the fact is your life is a mess. And I think I might be able to help you with it. That is, if you're brave enough to try."

Wes looked down, thunderstruck.

"Why don't you go home and think about it," I said, walking toward the door, even though there was time left in the hour. "If you wish to quit," I went on, standing at the door, looking him in the eye, "it's your decision and yours alone. You go home and think on it. If you are quitting, please leave me a message on the machine." I handed him a card and saw Wes out.

Wes never called though I never expected he'd make the effort of calling to cancel. His resistance to seeing and dealing with all the reality that was bearing down on him was easy to grasp. But then, I'd learned early that I can't do therapy *for* a child. When he didn't show up, I waited 30 minutes before calling it over. No surprise, I thought, as I headed out for a coffee. I opened the front door and a breathless Wes ran into me. "Sorry," he said. "My mom's car wouldn't start but we got a jump from my uncle." "No problem," I replied, happy he came, glad I was wrong.

What do therapists do with an adolescent patient's resistance? They try to understand it, and hold onto what they know about the teenager and the progress she's made. They take care that they don't use it as an excuse to reject a child or escape a difficult treatment. They try something to help the patient open up, perhaps asking the adolescent to keep a journal or correspond via e-mail. Therapists might disclose something about themselves that, they think, might buoy the teen patient, offer hope, or help her know that she isn't the only one coping with such difficulty. A lighter or casual mood can sometimes unseat a weighty mood that won't budge. Therapists will beware that the adolescent's therapeutic quagmire is not a response to some lack of empathy or optimism in the therapist.

"It's the car that got stuck, it's the mud, it's the mud," the Brazilian songwriter Antonio Carlos Jobim wrote in his beautiful, *Waters of March*. Jobim knew that a life is full of moments when nothing good happens, or when nothing happens at all. So it is with even the best of therapies. The clinician's goal cannot be to prevent such moments from happening, but to recognize them when they come and to treat them with the respect, hope, and creativity due any other aspect of therapy.

16

SOW'S EARS, SILK PURSES, AND SILVER LININGS

Finding Opportunity in Crisis

Crisis: A word to shudder the spine of any therapist. Images of people on the windowsill of the Empire State Building or alone in their room holding a bottle of antidepressants. This is one instance where the Hollywood version has probably been too neat and sanitized. As therapists we know all too well the realities of crisis, what it really looks like. Do enough therapy and you will know plenty of crises, maybe enough to ruin your sleep or push you toward early retirement or another career.

Crisis management refers to a focus on ways of dealing with the inevitable crisis that comes every therapist's way. For better or worse and to a large degree, *management* has come to hold as much legal as clinical implications. Workshops are commonly presented that show clinicians how to reduce their liability when treating at-risk patients. Unfortunately, this has left therapists somewhat alone on a branch when deciding what's therapeutically best for their patients. And ironically, when legal or health system considerations override the best interests of the patient, therapists' vulnerability actually goes up. This chapter explains various aspects of crisis. In the end, I hope to lend therapists greater confidence in their ability to manage crisis as therapeutically as possible.

COPING WITH SUICIDAL IMPULSES AND THINKING

When therapists who work with adolescents think crisis, they think suicide. Therapists who worry about it are not imagining a false danger. The threat is real. Suicide is the third leading cause of death in America's youth. And yet, suicidal thinking is everywhere. Work with teen-agers and you will learn that many, if not most of them sometimes wonder whether living is worth it. For reasons beyond this book, today's adolescents, when overtaxed by situations or feelings, are prone to consider suicide a viable alternative. How can therapists judge the seriousness of suicidal intent, and what can they do with it?

> *"I'm going to kill myself. All I do is fuck everything up and piss everybody off. Everybody is sick of me."*

What Roscoe said wasn't untrue. He'd stolen from his parents, failed in school, gotten in trouble with the law, and made life hard for his family. His mishaps and frequent legal needs had consumed much of his parents' savings.

> *"I'm going to drive my car into a tree, that will be the easiest way."* Roscoe couldn't look at me, nor could he cry.
> *I waited and watched.*
> *"I'm going to floor the gas and gun it right into the giant oak down my street."*

At this point, conventional wisdom of suicide assessment would have suggested that I stop the idle chitchat, put on my psychiatric equivalent of an EMT hat, get the clinical sirens whining, and the strobe lights flashing. Emergency! In my experience, nothing, and I mean nothing, risks taking me further from the clinical truth and rightful action. To abuse an already overdone metaphor, it's as if I rush my ambulance so fast and frantically that I drive right past the accident victim.

My thinking about crisis sharpened during my first clinical job after graduate school. I was a general clinician at a community mental health center attached to a general hospital and one of my tasks was to provide psychiatric coverage to the emergency room two days a week. The ambulance or police would bring in a suicidal person and I'd have an hour or less to figure it out. Green behind the ears, I'd follow the prescribed regimen for suicidal assessment and ask lots of pointed questions about the suicidal intent, plan, and so on. By the end of the hour, I'd usually feel as lost as when I'd begun. *Was this person going to kill himself?* Hell, if I knew.

But slowly, I discovered something. The more I allowed myself to sit back and listen with curiosity and caring, as if doing therapy, the more I'd learn about the patient's suicidality. "Why there?" I once asked a suicidal man who'd stressed that he would sever his wrists in the kitchen. "So *she'll* trip on me when she comes home." That seemingly irrelevant question led to a rich outpouring of rage toward a mother who'd forever criticized her 45-year-old bachelor son. Instead of suicide or hospitalization, we agreed to some outpatient family work that quickly helped this odd couple achieve some harmony in their home. That lesson led the way with Roscoe.

"Why the oak?" I asked.

"My parents love that fucking tree. They think it's fucking perfect."

"Jealous of a tree," I said.

Roscoe crumpled down into the chair.

This may sound unrealistic. It happened. I've seen it happen many times in my practice. A teenager talks of suicide, even with a plan, and yet my attention to one small detail takes us to a whole other place, to the deeper feelings and reasons behind the wish to die. In my experience giving someone a third-degree about their plan seldom seems to reduce the pain or desperation. In Roscoe's case, his revelations led to shedding of great pain and a new conviction that maybe talking in therapy could bring him relief.

When I start out with adolescents who've already tried to commit suicide, I work hard to quickly create a robust framework and holding space. I do not casually slide into therapy with actively suicidal teens. I put a heavy obligation on them and their parents:

"If we are going to work together, we need to have some basic things understood and agreed on. You, to the best of your ability, have to keep me informed of suicidal feelings. Do you understand that?" I'll ask, looking at the adolescent. "I do not want you running at the emergency room or making suicidal gestures," I will say in those exact words. "Please, call me first, then we can decide what to do." I stop at every sentence and make sure that everyone is with me.

"When you try to hurt yourself or do something else like cut yourself or drink, we lose an opportunity. That's when you are hurting the most, and that's when we can finally

*learn what's eating at you. If you go and cut or OD or some-
thing, we'll never find out!"*

*Finally, I urge them (almost demand) that when they see
a crisis coming on, they call, whenever it is, and we'll meet
as quickly as we can. I do not ask them to sign a paper, but I
do shake their hands, look them in the eye, and let them know
I am very serious about helping them.*

Of course, if my words were just a come-on, I'd be putting
myself in a very perilous position, one unethical and highly un-
fair to the adolescent. I'd better be willing to deliver on my
end, whether it's seeing them on a weekend evening or being
willing to sit with their most extreme distress. But, as with my
willingness to e-mail patients, I find that being available in this
way has made my job more meaningful and satisfying. It also
enables me to stay in control of cases and to keep them contained in the outpatient setting and within the therapeutic
relationship.

Consider what happens in the hospital? Actually, the question is what doesn't happen? Everything. More than a thousand dollars per day of insurance coverage buys almost nothing
therapeutic. In a matter of days the hospital sends these patients off carrying hastily written and appalling discharge sum-
maries that add nothing to what was known prior to admission.
That money would have been so much better spent in a place
where the adolescent could heal, like being able to see her
therapist several times a week.

By my way of thinking, hospitalizing my patients risks making my work that much harder. Now, my task involves dealing
with the patient's possible feelings of stigma, fear, a sense of
powerlessness, and maybe her deciding that this means she is
too disturbed for outpatient therapy alone. She might see the

hospitalization as proof that she is incapable of controlling her own self-destructive impulses; and that is a terribly frightening and cruel burden to put on someone's shoulders, especially someone who is struggling to keep herself safe.

I much prefer, when it's possible and safe, to sit tight with patients' suicidal thinking. *"Your impulses to die and cut and destroy yourself,"* I make clear, *"can be said here without punishment and without fear."* Simply speaking their suicidal thoughts out loud in my presence (i.e., with someone who cares and is not scared) can help to tether a teenager to the world of the living. And who would you be more likely to explore and decipher your death wishes with—someone who welcomes them as part of you or someone who immediately dials the men in the white coats? We all know the answer.

I do not have an iron-clad strategy for assessing suicide in teenagers. It is an active process of listening within the context of an ongoing therapy and alongside the facts of a child's life. Every clinician has to confront his or her own sensibilities, anxieties, and limitations. Knowing oneself as a clinician has no more essential place than when working with suicidal youth. I've even heard some therapists say they refuse to work with suicidal people (though I do not know how one could even arrange that). Don't most thinking people have moments of doubt?

For those of you who hold greater belief or have had experiences that convince you of the necessity to hospitalize suicidal teens, I offer some cautions. One, wait until you've secured an inpatient bed before telling reluctant teens and families that the hospital is needed. Otherwise, should you not find a bed, you'll send them home to keep safe after having just convinced them of their inability to do so. Two, written contracts to keep oneself safe, especially with patients we know well, can be counterproductive. A sincere, "Can I trust you to stay safe?"

will probably have more impact on a hurting teenager than some fake legal document that lacks the personal touch. Again, let me ask, what will likely help you not to hurt yourself: signing a pathetic contract written in pseudolegalese, or a sincere, spoken, eye-to-eye and heartfelt agreement. "I know it's going to be hard, but I'll see you again first thing in the morning."

Needless to say, my approach reflects a bias, a subjective conglomeration of my clinical training, thinking, and experience. It is not *the* way to manage suicide; it is *my* way. All therapists must discover, learn, and ever refine their own ways of managing the crises sure to intrude on their clinical work, even on their most successful therapies. It is too important and sensitive an issue to leave to other people's judgment and doing.

MANAGING OTHER CRISES

While suicide is the greatest fear of therapists who work with teenagers, it is hardly the only crisis that presents itself. Work with enough teenagers, and you, as therapist, will encounter crises involving drugs, alcohol, self-injury, eating disorders, paralyzing depression, psychotic regressions, and calamitous school failure or refusal, to name the big few. Then, too, there are the problems that occur with the police and the courts. Obviously, there is no way that one book can responsibly address these issues with sufficient detail and care. I'd like, however, to discuss in general my methods of dealing with such difficult, if common, situations.

Sudden changes often signal something of clinical note, the what, why, and how of which needs to be examined and understood, especially in the context of the therapy and what has been the teen's functioning up to that point. Here, please know,

I do not refer to handling crises of adolescents you are just meeting in the emergency room. (Assessing and handling critical crisis in an adolescent you have never met is not the topic of this chapter or this book.) Why, I'll ask myself, has a teenage patient's symptom intensified, just appeared, or transformed into something seemingly more dangerous or worrisome? Does the apparent regression run parallel with what I've been seeing in therapy, or, in fact, does it contradict how well the therapy has been going? I'll ask teenage patients how they see it, how they explain the altered trajectory and discrepancy between how they are in my office and what is happening at home or school.

I caution myself to keep at least one foot out of the mayhem and to resist panic calls for action that parents, teachers, lawyers, and even the teenagers themselves send my way. I've seen a sudden crisis arise because a parent (unconsciously) doesn't want to deal with their child anymore. That sad circumstance may demand my intervention, but not in the exact ways that the parents would hope for (e.g., hospitalizing or placing in residential treatment, measures that take the teenager away and put them in somebody else's care and hair). Does the current exacerbation indicate the need for a new intervention or for a reconfiguration, ramping up, or rethinking of the current one, particularly the therapy? If the problem relates to the teenager's being overwhelmed by internal conflicts or feelings, especially those whose uncovering or sharpening is in the long run a good thing, increasing the frequency of therapy may be enough. When behaviors or distress cannot be managed by therapy alone, medication consultation and more substantial treatments must be considered.

Crises involving drugs and alcohol confront us with a more eclectic challenge. Though, at any one time, several of my teenage patients use alcohol or marijuana, I do go on alert when

I hear that their using has increased or broadened. Is the substance abuse something amenable to outpatient talking treatment, or, as was true in the case of an teenage girl who binge drank herself into oblivion and dangerous situations, does it require detox, rehab, or treatment that is based on behavioral techniques or the model of Alcoholics or Narcotics Anonymous? Seldom, in my experience, does talk alone rein in utterly uncontrolled drinking or drug use; in fact, too much affect can make it worse.

Crises of misbehavior, such as getting in trouble for breaking the law, are a related but different group of problems. Here, therapists must step warily, keeping the clinical focus in clear view. What, I ask myself, does this problem mean for the adolescent's therapy and growth? What is called for legally does not always equate with what the teenager needs clinically. Given the adolescent's recent improvement in self-control and behavior, do I want to advocate for the court's leniency? Or, do I judge that the teen needs to feel the consequences of his unrepentant deeds? I am happy to intercede when I feel it will help the adolescent; I am loathe to intervene when I feel it will mostly indulge and excuse a teenager's already undeveloped conscience. It is the teenager's clinical needs that move me, not parents' desperate pleas that I protect their young criminal from the punishments he's brought on himself.

I am especially vigilant to signs of brewing crisis: faces and moods that grow darker and removed; rigid smiles and saccharine "Fine's" that betray lives falling apart; repeated and seemingly unavoidable close calls with cars, police, sex, and the like; increased fascination with self-injurious behaviors; and, signs suggesting abuse or neglect at home. In these situations, I try my best to get proactive, even if within the steady context of the therapy as we have known it. When their lives get harder, and they feel less safe and more alone, our teenage patients need us more than ever to be dependable, reliable, and available. Many times, fortifying my therapeutic presence facilitates the teenager's coming forth, filling me in, and working more cooperatively with me to come up with a doable and useful therapeutic plan.

A crisis can signal therapy gone bad, therapy gone good, and therapy not enough, just as it can have nothing at all to do with treatment. The best we as therapists can do, it seems, is to put out the fire and initiate damage control quickly, transforming the crisis into containable behavior and conflict that can be brought back into the therapy as soon as possible.

EMBRACING AND EXPLOITING
THERAPEUTIC CRISIS

There is crisis, and then there's what I call *therapeutic* crisis. An example of a crisis would be a child who's not in therapy making a suicide attempt. An instance of a therapeutic crisis would be a child who's in therapy, talking more openly and with plans about her wish to do herself in. The main difference, as is probably obvious, is whether or not the "crisis" behavior or change occurs within or outside of a sound therapy.

> *"I want to die." Athena's eyes were closed and she spoke softly. "I can't bear it any longer." She sat unnervingly still, as if every last molecule of energy had been drained from her body. Dark rings circled her eyes. She couldn't cry.*

Athena had been depressed for some time. She'd stopped doing schoolwork and had withdrawn from peers. She'd stopped eating for a short while, and then went the other way, eating too much. Though everyone could see her depression, she'd barely acknowledged it, coming in each week talking of feeling blah and not much more. Previous sessions consisted mostly of updates, spoken in a monotonous tone: "I ate a bit less"; "I tried walking today but I got tired"; "I'm flunking history now, too." I'd follow up with confirming nods, open-ended questions, and more probing ones. "No"; "Not really"; "I don't know." She'd make clear her lack of interest in thinking about any one of them. We spent a lot of time sitting in heavy silence.

"It really hurts," I said.

Appearing to use her last bit of strength, Athena nodded her head.

At the hour's end Athena shook my hand, something she'd never done. "Thanks for everything," she said.

Was that a "good-bye world, forever" gesture, she left me wondering.

Athena went home and told her parents that she was going to starve to death, and in fact, she did cut her eating to Saltines and water for a few days. Her parents, frightened, pushed for hospitalization, but I suggested we stay the course. Strange as it may sound, Athena's great and dark pain and beginning to talk about how she'd kill herself encouraged me. For one, she was talking—morbidly but with feeling, even if it was a heavy sadness, but that sadness felt more alive than anything I'd ever sensed in her. Two, she was connecting with me, again, even if around her plan to slowly kill herself. Three, her suicide plan intrigued me; while proposed as a way of killing herself, it was getting her weight back to where she'd wanted it to be. Her hours grew more morbid. And then, at the end of another dismal session in which she'd eerily described watching her own funeral, she said something that lingered and worried me throughout the afternoon. "I'm not sure I can wait," she'd said.

By the time I called her parents, they'd already left a message for me to call them. Fortunately, they went first. They'd seen a big change. She'd come home from her hour and had made herself a sandwich that she ate while listening to music. They didn't want to jinx it, but they felt that maybe she was turning for the better. How did I explain it? I didn't have to. Athena did. Over many hours she described how she'd used therapy to share her self-hatred and how she'd taken some pleasure in making me and her parents lose sleep over her.

"Thanks for not putting me in the hospital," she said.
"Thanks for believing in me." Athena could finally cry.

In my work, almost every therapy with a significantly troubled teen encounters one or more crises. Those adolescents have taught me not to view those predicaments and regressions as irreversible disasters or even as signs of failure or deterioration. I've come to see them as moments of great meaning, signaling a need of attention. Maybe, I'll find, it is calling for some extra therapy, an intervention at home, or is underlining some countertransference of my own that is getting in the way. Maybe it's a developmental need to see me upset, worried, inconvenienced—all for them. Whatever its underlying meaning, I usually find that these crises become golden opportunities to move the therapy and child ahead, oftentimes in new, bigger, and better ways.

KNOW YOURSELF

In closing, I need to mention two matters that can be highly relevant and critical. As therapists we wield more power and persuasion than we may recognize. Like the wizards of fantasy, we can use our powers for good or evil. Though we know we don't intend to do evil, there are times when we can provoke more than we can handle. When working with a fragile teen, particularly one feeling suicidal, we do best by going slowly. Cornering an adolescent, who is not seeing any way out, can leave him no other option but to escape through self-harm, injury, or death that may be murderously targeted at those who'd hurt, abandoned, or neglected him. Imagine being a suicidal teen, feeling that no one in the world gets it, yet having to find solace with a therapist who, acting like just another deputy of the parent-school-law axis, gets in your face with dares to grow up and get over it. Sadly, I've seen adolescents who were "pushed" by supposed helpers into self-destructive places. Of course, we know who bears the blame afterward, it's the child.

Similarly, a self-destructive adolescent can take its toll on parents, caretakers, and therapists. If you are committed to such a child, use colleagues, consultation, training, or your own therapy to help keep your vision clear and centered. Know your limits, too. If these kinds of cases do you in, or feel too much, stay away from them. For when you become overwhelmed or exhausted, you may pull away from the therapy and the child, leaving him abandoned, or you may grow susceptible to quick and dirty referrals to any place or intervention that will take him somewhere else. These are not flattering and happy images, I know, but they are real.

17

FAILURES, MISSTEPS, AND LOST CAUSES

Learning and Recovering from the Inevitable

Doing therapy defines imperfection. There are few absolute rules. Every patient, situation, and moment is unique. The decisions therapists make are less black-and-white and more a thousand shades of gray. Therapists often operate in a kind of black hole where, for the most part, they rely on what they see and hear in a contained space and time to "know" what goes on the other six days and 23-plus hours of their patients' lives. Interventions are approximations, therapists' best educated guesses at what might help their adolescent patients given what their history, experience, and clinical model predict. It's as if there were dozens of schools of thought on how to treat a broken leg, and then, as if the legs had different levels of motivation on being treated and getting better. Only that's far too simplistic compared to the therapist's job of making such judgments every minute of every hour, judgments that are ever a compromise between the ideal and real, what we think we understand and what we don't, what patients are saying and what they're not. Clinicians who work on the front lines in clinics, community health centers, HMOs, and the like, work an even more impossible job as they are forced to do all of the above with more patients in less time and with less support. The stresses and human element of this profession dooms therapists to a great deal of failure and disappointment.

TRY NOT TO SCARE OFF PATIENTS

When starting my private practice, one of my first referrals was for a high school senior described to me by his mother as bright and wanting to talk with a therapist. In that phone call, she mentioned depression, loneliness, and, what had prompted her contacting me: Gideon was going out late every night and not coming back until the early morning. She said her son worked during the day and had plenty of money. She feared he was spending it on drugs or maybe even prostitutes, though knowing his shyness, she couldn't imagine that. "I ask him where he goes," she'd said. "But he tells me he's an adult and it's none of my business." Gideon had always been a good boy, and he was almost 19, so his mother felt she had to respect his privacy. "I know it's not your job," she'd said at the end of our call, "but if there's any way you can find out where he goes and what he's doing, at least tell me that he's safe."

Did I ever look forward to this case of an intelligent young man who wanted help, and best of all, who was living a mystery. As one who always saw the therapist as a sort of Sherlock Holmes of the mind, I was, excuse the expression, psyched. On the day of his first meeting I was prepared to meet the case of my yet young career.

Gideon did not let me down. He was a large, smart, and articulate, if reserved, 18-year-old who spoke with a lisp. "I just want help with not feeling so down," he said in our first few minutes. "I hope you can help me. Though I know I'll have to do my share in here, too," he'd quickly added. Gideon wanted help, and he even had a sense of the work that therapy involves. We spent the hour going over his distress and his history. He and his mother lived about an hour north in an old New England town. His parents had divorced a couple of years ago and his father had moved to Boston. Gideon told me what a great guy his dad was and how they loved spending time together.

I listened for clues to where Gideon went at night. I heard none. I asked him if he wished to give therapy a try. He replied that he didn't need to try it, he was sure he wanted it. We spent some time scheduling an hour that we agreed would be Gideon's permanently. Later that day, once my enthusiasm had settled down, I recalled meeting Gideon and just how unhappy he'd appeared. I felt glad that I'd had this awakening, and renewed my own vow to help him feel better as fast as I could.

"You look tired," I said early into Gideon's second hour. I saw eyes that looked troubled and as if they hadn't slept for days.

"I stay up kind of late," he answered.

"Doing what?" I asked.

"I go out at night."

"Where do you go?"

"Boston."

"Boston? At night, that's pretty far away. How do you get here?"

"I take the train."

"How long does that take?"

"About 70 minutes each way."

"What do you do in Boston?"

"Stuff."

"What kind of stuff?"

"I walk around."

"Where do you walk?"

"I just walk around?"

"You just walk around?"

I'll spare you rest of the hour's misery. I fancied myself the detective of 221B Baker Street; I behaved like the guy from *Dragnet*. All I was missing in my interrogation of Gideon was the lone, unshaded light bulb hanging over his head. At the hour's end, frustrated, I said we would continue this next time. Gideon left with a halfhearted, "Sure thing."

When Gideon didn't show up the following week, I called his home. His mother answered and, to my surprise, she sounded much better. She told me how she'd meant to call me. Gideon had told her that I'd helped him get back on track and that he was going to take a break from therapy for now. Oh, and he'd also told her where he went at night. With a choked voice, she described that he'd been going into Boston to look for his father, a schizophrenic man who drove an all-night taxicab and who had never told Gideon where he'd moved. Gideon, she said, "walked the streets of Boston night after night, hailing cabs, looking in vain for his father. "Well, I know he isn't doing heroin. I thank you for that."

His mother had gotten some fast relief, and Gideon, in the way that I imagined he did when thinking of his father, had protected my image for his mother. But I knew the truth of how my 21-question assault had chased Gideon away. I knew he'd keep looking for his father. But I wondered if he'd ever try looking for a therapist again, and that seemed a greater tragedy.

KNOW YOUR LIMITATIONS

Belief in one's abilities can be good, but knowing one's limitations is better. Early in my career I thought I could handle al-

most anything. Like a high priest of Ninja who fends off flying swords and kicking feet with grace and lightning speed, I
welcomed any therapeutic challenge.

> *"I don't give a fuck." Matt adjusted his earphones and
> turned the volume up. I could hear deafening heavy metal
> reverberating through his head.*
> *"Kind of loud?"*
> *Matt didn't hear me.*
> *"Your court date is Friday and you don't give a fuck that
> you have a second offense to report?"*
> *Matt pulled out a cigarette and walked outside. He came
> back a few minutes later, sat down, and put a new CD in his
> Walkman.*
> *"Is that a new CD player?"*
> *"He nodded.*
> *"Stole it?" I asked, knowing the answer.*
> *He nodded and laughed. "You want me to get you one?"*

It would be self-abusive to show you my many sessions with
Matt. Even beginners would probably wonder what I was
thinking. I knew about the stealing, drugs, alcohol, unsafe sex,
cheating, and lying that never took a break. Not that I haven't
worked with such problems and seen growth. But with Matt,
there was nothing to grab onto. He showed no remorse, no suffering, no motivation at all. He showed no internal change, and
that is what usually compels me to keep working with such a
case. I sometimes would take his offering me something stolen
as a sign of affection or attachment or something positive, but
it wasn't. Every session was as inert as the last, that is, when he
bothered to show up. Matt's parents were lawyers who wanted
outpatient therapy to work. They cared about their image in the

community and did not want anything messy or blemishing. I wanted to think that I could deliver that. To make a painfully long story short, I'd unknowingly strung Matt through arrests, court appearances, school suspensions, and expulsion not to mention the death-defying recklessness of his daily life. I finally surrendered, though I occasionally receive calls asking if I'll fill out some form or other to support another round of rehabilitation or detox.

My intentions were genuine. I wanted to help Matt restore his life. I kidded myself mostly as to what I saw. He was beyond my skills and understanding and talents. Now when I meet such a child, I am careful not to take on more than my skills and understanding can do. I know that clinicians older and wiser than me, perhaps even younger and wiser, have learned this lesson more easily than I did. I know also they might be the first to assure me that I was doing the best I could. Would earlier and more intensive treatment have made a difference? That question touches on one of the curses of doing therapy: we'll never know.

STICK TO WHAT YOU KNOW IS RIGHT

A school counselor had made the referral of what he called the strangest case he'd ever seen, a high school junior who wouldn't come to school. The oddest piece for the counselor came when he, the principal, and the town's truant officer came to Lynda's house to bring her to school as her family and the special education team had agreed. He told of going to the child's home and the mother's leading them into the girl's bedroom where she slept soundly. The school team woke her. She asked for 15 minutes to get ready. After a half an hour of waiting in the living room, they discovered that Lynda had gone back to sleep. "Talk about blowing someone off," the counselor said with a chuckle.

Late into her scheduled hour, I heard the beeping of a truck. I looked outside to see two girls on either end of my driveway, gesturing and yelling, directing a truck as it backed into my driveway. I called to them but they paid no attention to me. They spent many minutes guiding the truck to my door.

The driver, Lynda's father, climbed out of the cabin, gave me a curt and obligatory nod, and asked me where the office was as if delivering a couch to my home. Amazed by the whole scene, I pointed the way. He went into the cabin, lifted the truck's sliding door, put down a heavy ramp, and wheeled an enormous and heavy television into my office. The girls followed with a Nintendo console, various joysticks, and a canvas bag of games. The three of them, wholly oblivious to my presence, moved my desk to make room for the television, unplugged lamps to free up outlets, and lay on the floor and wired the system.

When the system was set, one girl, who I presumed was Lynda, took a joystick and with her back to me began playing a racing game. "I'll be back in a couple of hours," her father said. "Gee, I'm sorry. We only have five minutes left," I replied. "But I have a little time before my next person. We can go fifteen minutes" I offered, thinking the extra time might help me get the therapy going.

As you guessed by now, Lynda played her game and ignored me. At the hour's end, my next patient and I stood in the driveway, out of the way, waiting and watching as Lynda and her entourage moved her gaming equipment back into the truck.

"Gee," the next hour's 10-year-old quipped. "My mother told me not to bring my harmonica until I asked you if it was okay."

Give me a break, I already felt stupid enough. I'd never witnessed anything like that and was taken totally by surprise. But even had Lynda or her family asked, I then probably would have said, sure, seeing it as a possible avenue to engaging her in treatment. You know by now that I never saw Lynda again (not that we ever really met). When her father returned a few days later to pick up cables they'd left behind, he said it all in a mutter meant for me. "What a waste that was. She needs a therapist to play video games. She can do that at home."

In retrospect, what would I do now? I'd take charge of the referral. What, I'd prominently note, must be going on inside the head and home of a child who can comfortably fall back to sleep with her teachers in the next room? I'd be more worried than bemused. And I'd have made that clear by gently but firmly stopping the truck, blocking the television, inviting Lynda and her father inside, and talking to them about the realities of Lynda's plight and what therapy might do to help. There's a good reason why my office doesn't have a string of grounded outlets and a 48-inch screen or even a smaller one. And I'd also have enforced the boundaries of Lynda's scheduled meeting rather than run into my next patient's hour. Though I now continue to smile and joke with new patients and their families, I seldom forget the sober reasons that we meet.

BEWARE OF FRUSTRATION

Micah was a handsome, athletic, and highly intelligent 12-year-old referred to me, so his mother said, as a last resort. They'd been seen by several senior and well-known clinicians in Boston, none of whom seemed to help. "There are a lot of quacks in your profession," Micah's mother said with not a hint of self-doubt. "Are you a quack?" she asked me. I laughed and said, that, I thought I could help them. We were all happy with my unbridled confidence and settled on a course of therapy. We quickly established a pattern. Micah came to his hours happy, cordial, and flattering, after which his mother would call me and tell me what a little con artist he was and how he'd just stolen this or lied about that. She blamed Micah's father, an executive, for their son's lack of moral fiber. "Life is just one big lie," she said, referring to her ex-husband. I'd confront Micah in the next hour and he'd confess, then later that day his mother would again call and tell me how I'd been had once more.

I met with Micah's father alone, his mother alone, with both parents, and with the whole family. Everyone called everyone a liar; and, it seemed that they were all right. I seldom heard the same story the same way twice, even from the same mouth. Micah's parents told me he'd paid another boy to do a term paper and how he'd paid a girl to make out with him or "whatever else they did." In their words, they feared his becoming a "little sociopath" who would grow up to be a big one. And yet, as I wondered aloud with them, they never seemed to do anything that might help Micah learn right from wrong. I'd suggest consequences and structure to force Micah to live more honestly. They never complied with our plan even while complaining more loudly about his deceptions. My frustration reached its peak when they called me during my family vacation. "We know you're away but this is really urgent. Please call!"

I called and Micah's mother told me that he'd stolen several hundred dollars from an elderly neighbor, a lovely woman who regularly gave the boy gifts, food, and an occasional dollar to buy himself treats. What incited Micah's mother was the evil she now saw in Micah's scheming. He'd actually visited the woman on the day he knew she cashed her social security check. He'd feigned hunger, knowing she'd make him something to eat. While she cooked for him, he emptied her pocketbook. I swallowed my fury at Micah and his parents, and agreed to meet the first day I'd be home.

When we met, I was pleased to see how distressed and angry Micah's parents were. They'd gotten it. They said they'd do anything it took now, for they saw Micah was headed to a life of jail or worse. I suggested a stern plan. Micah was to pay back every penny plus interest. He was not to take the money from his sizable savings account, but was to earn it through hard work for meager wages. They suggested ten dollars an hour for working harder on his homework. I suggested one dollar an hour for hard labor, cleaning out the basement, and scraping and painting the part of their old barn that he could reach. "How will we know he is really working?" his mother asked. "By watching him," I replied. "They'll never stick to it," Micah said with a sly smile. "I'll bet you a dollar they forget about it in a few days." But his parents didn't waver. They made clear a new regime had begun.

It didn't take but a few days before Micah's mother called to tell me he'd been caught cheating at school, and that she was washing her hands of the boy. I asked how the payback was going. She laughed. "There's no way I'm going to stand over him like some prison guard. I've got a life, too." When she asked me what I planned to do about Micah's latest caper, I replied that I was going to resign. And I did.

At the time I felt justified, while also foolish that I thought I could do something no one else had been able to do. Now, I have other ideas. I abandoned the boy just like his parents had. They were ambivalent at best about having him, and I did little better. That's what I'd notice and address if I could meet that family today.

LET IT GO

Like every therapist, I've had my failures, many of which I've helped to create. But there have been others when nothing and no one could do more. Are there really any lost causes? It is horrible to think there are, and yet, look over your own past and present caseloads. What is your view?

The answer, perhaps, is best found and left in the pudding. I hope there are always other clinicians who will see some twinkle, something salvageable in the teenagers that we are unable to help. I hope also that those children will try one more time to get the help they need and deserve. In the meanwhile, therapists can try to live by the credo they hold out for their patients: *do the best you can and forgive yourself when you fall short*. Learning from our mistakes is healthy and constructive; beating ourselves senseless over them is something else.

18

HELPING HANDS

Working with Parents

Therapists and their patients' parents have an unusual relationship. Feeling inadequate and vulnerable, and frequently with great effort, they bring their children to us. In return, we offer them hope, but at a cost. In practical terms we depend on parents to bring their children, call ahead to cancel and change appointments, and pay the bills or show us their insurance cards. But we ask a lot more of them. We want them to support their teenager's therapy by making it a priority in the family schedule as high or higher than the orthodontist, drum teacher, and hair stylist. We want parents to be involved, and yet ask that they respect the privacy of therapy. By doing so we imply that they blindly trust what we do behind closed doors with their child, even as we push them to grow more involved and vigilant over the rest of their child's life. We ask, too, that they subject themselves to our therapeutic ways, that they be treated alongside their adolescents. Ever strive to grow as parents, we ask of them, just as we ask that they work to better create the space for their children to change for the better. Given how much parents mean to our work and patients, shouldn't we take a closer look?

WELCOME PARENTS

Telling a therapist, *"Our child needs help and so do we,"* is not easy, and can represent an act of great love and caring. Coming to our office and admitting that things are not well can feel deeply shaming, sad, and disappointing. Few parents envision a psychoanalytic couch when dreaming about their baby's tomorrow. All parents want to get it right and they want to be able to do it on their own, without professional assistance. That, in the course of their child's therapy, those parents will likely have to show and confront the ugliest moments of their home life only makes their heads hang lower. Calling it a narcissistic injury belittles the anguish parents can feel when crossing our doorsteps. Though the power of therapy may eventually help restore or even better a child's future, in that awful beginning, a parent can only feel that the damage has been done, that their child has been ruined. And any parent knows that there isn't any greater pain than that of believing you've somehow hurt your child and risked her chance for happiness and health.

When I meet parents, I forever put myself in their place. I assume there's always more beneath the initial small talk, smiles, and laughter. Let them show me over time that they don't care about or hurt over their child. Loving, until proven otherwise, is the law of my therapeutic land. I try my best to make them feel welcome, comfortable, and heard on our first meeting. Although I may already have heard "bad" things about their parenting and characters—I try to meet with my new adolescent patients first—I try to reopen my mind. After all, teenagers give me one perspective and the parents usually have another or two. It doesn't take a lifetime of doing therapy, or even being a psychologist, to know that the truth lies somewhere between.

What are their concerns? What do they want me to know about their child, about themselves? What is their biggest worry about this whole, complicated situation? My agenda runs a distant second to the parents' idea of what we should address. I may think it's their son's sadness over the grandmother's death; they may judge it's the way he's fresh at home. I leave plenty of room for their distraction and digressions, only gently corralling them when we go too far astray, as can happen with a highly disorganized parent. I stop and pause when their distress overwhelms them or when they appear to be thinking where our discussion should go next.

> *Neither parent had said anything nice about their daughter. I'd heard lots as to how bitchy, self-centered, lazy, mean, lying, and unpleasant she could be, and our time was running out.*
>
> *"And despite all that, you're still worried about her," I said quietly. Neither parent replied. I waited.*
>
> *"She says she wants to die," the mother suddenly blurted with an aching gush. "My baby wants to kill herself." The mother fell into her husband's shoulders, sobbing. He looked to the ceiling, straining to hold back his own tears.*

Parents' wish that we hear them is neither selfish nor idle. *"If you can't listen or meet me where I am,"* they've told me, *"how can you do the same for my child?"*

GET PARENTS ON BOARD

I typically don't believe in reading riot acts before the riot. I do, however, work to make the ground rules of therapy clear as quickly as the circumstances of our first meetings allow. I neither pronounce a list of do's and don't's nor do I offer handouts detailing them. I strive to make them evident and tangibly memorable by demonstrating them in action. Rather than state the need for them to get their child to me on time, I give my best effort to finding an hour that suits the child and her family, apologizing when I am unable to do so perfectly. Saying something like, "Tuesday at 3 o'clock will be Rachel's hour," can accomplish as much as a lecture on the importance of being earnest (about appointment times). Nor do I say much more than a casual and brief mention of how often and long we will meet and how billing works. Again, how we conduct ourselves will tell parents more about how we do business than any verbal brochure can.

In our first parent meeting, with the foreshadowing intent of an overture, I strive to demonstrate first-hand all that I will be doing with them. I smile, I laugh, I am serious. I listen carefully and patiently. On the other hand, I do not shy away from asking necessary questions: *Has your child ever been been abused physically or sexually? Have you ever wondered or worried that they have? Do you or any one else in the home use alcohol or drugs? How much?* And I pursue points of interest, just as I would with their child.

"At least we don't have to worry where she is at night," a mother said. She glanced at her husband and he, I could see, sucked in his lip not to laugh. These parents had spent most of this first hour blaming the junior high school and her teachers for all of their daughter's anxiety problems. "Anyway she's managing to get good grades," the mother continued.

"What is it?" I asked, wondering what the private joke had been about. Neither parent answered. I looked to them both and waited.

"She kind of has this sleeping problem," the father began sheepishly.

"Kind of a problem? She sleeps with us every night," the mother said.

"She didn't sleep with us Tuesday night."

"Adam had friends sleeping over. She was too embarrassed."

"Maybe we'd be better off just having more sleepovers." The father turned his side to me.

"You mean, better than doing therapy."

"Well, yeah, nothing personal, you seem like an all right guy. But, who wants to be doing this, really?"

"Not too many people, I suspect," I said with a smile. Both parents laughed.

My attending to a slight bump in the road brought several benefits: the parents could tell me about their daughter's intense separation anxiety; they also shared their shame about her "condition" as they called it; they raised the ways they disagree about parenting and the frequent arguments that arise; and it allowed the father to admit his misgivings about therapy, which, seeing that I accepted it, in turn, helped him to engage with me and the treatment. Our interactions gave the parents a living example of what I and the therapy would be like, how it would work. And last, they actually left our first meeting with something substantial in their hands; that is, a greater understanding of their child and themselves as her parents.

I also try to show parents how the lines of communication will work. Rather than talk in the abstract about confidentiality, I talk to the parents without sharing what their child has told me in confidence. What better way to make the privacy of therapy clear to them. Seeing me not betray their child similarly can persuade them that I will treat what they say with the same respect and insulation. My keeping true to the child also shows the parents that I am not afraid to stand up to them, that I'll do clinically what is best for their child even if it offends or disturbs them. Most loving parents come to value that.

In words and actions I want parents to be able to be as honest as they possibly can with me. How do I convince parents that it is worthwhile and safe enough to do so? I try to attend to the smaller things they tell me. If I can't pass that trial, do I deserve to be trusted with more important information? I hold judgment. If this career has taught me anything, it's that I usually don't know what it's like to walk in another parent's shoes. What, I want to know, are this mother's or father's *good reasons* for how they parent? I try not to fall out of my chair or to go for the jugular. If a parent's cautious disclosure leads to my overeager probing, they'll know better than to talk next time.

BE AVAILABLE AND FLEXIBLE

A majority of parents who bring their children to therapists are stressed. If we expect them to work at parenting, we need to be realistic about their resources and abilities. We also need to make ourselves as available as we can because it is at our urging somewhat that they are trying out new ways of behaving with their adolescents. "E-mail or call me," I say to parents who, I know, are attempting a new strategy they've never done before. "Don't spend the weekend fretting that it's gone downhill," I'll emphasize. "A two-minute call and I can probably help you get back on track."

"She's in the basement screaming and throwing things. We did what we talked about and now she's threatening to kill herself."

Cynthia's parents were trying their best. They'd weathered two suicide attempts before meeting me and understandably feared pushing their 15-year-old daughter over the edge. But she'd been doing much better. She'd returned to school and was engaged and learning well. Good friendships had resumed. And yet, she still held her parents hostage, with some justification, for her inner misery. "She needs more limits," I'd told them, "not in order to be a good girl," for she was one, "but to have a solid place to rail against."

So, that weekend they had resolved to plant their feet. And they had. They'd told their daughter that she couldn't go to the school dance until she'd neatened the basement playroom, a room that she'd ransacked over several months. Now, in the eleventh hour, their knees were weakening, and her father, Ed, had called me. "Hang in there, Ed," was about all I had to say. Less than an hour later, he called back.

> *"She just came to us and politely asked us to see the base-ment. She'd cleaned it beautifully. We kind of want to let her go for the last hour of the dance, do you think that's bad?"* Cynthia's father asked me.
>
> *"What's your call?"* I asked.
>
> *"To let her go,"* he replied.
>
> *"I'd listen to your advice, it's pretty good,"* I said, more relieved and encouraged about Cynthia than I'd ever been.

But all he needed was my ear to bounce his fear off and to confirm his sound reasoning as to why Cynthia was safe, and that they'd done right by her. Less than five minutes on the telephone helped Cynthia's parents follow through on the big and hard work they'd been doing in their meetings with me.

My flexibility also implies that I can be accommodating as to whom I meet with in any one session. From the beginning, I "train" the parents I work with to expect that I may ask to meet with any one of them at any time. As I said earlier in the book, when I see something inescapable in the waiting room, I am apt to invite the parents along with the teenager. If they behave like that in front of their therapist, mustn't they be asking that their behavior be noticed and maybe, even that their therapist do something? I regularly meet families in all sorts of configurations as clinical moments dictate. Should a pink elephant appear on my threshold, I cannot help but let it in. If I hear about police trouble, court appearances, physical fights, I invite the parents in with the adolescent. Meetings between parent and child can powerfully reduce conflict and initiate some reparation and healing. When there is a big decision to make, I may ask that the adolescent bring his parents with him. In that meeting, I'll make clear that we are not meeting to wage a therapeutic battle. I'll ask that they down their swords just long enough to make a good mutual decision in the child's best interest. To my amazement, and in spite of the strife, parents and child often are able to reach practical solutions and see threads of connection, harmony, and love that none of them knew existed.

HELP PARENTS TAKE THEIR TEEN'S PERSPECTIVE

My reasons and methods of confronting teens and their parents are basically the same: to help them see, feel, or understand something that isn't quite seen or understood.

"Why don't you just buy him a gun?" I asked, tempering my sarcasm as much as I could.

Harry's parents said nothing, believing, so it looked, that
they were watching their son's therapist go crazy.

Harry's parents had the patience of saints. Some people
would use other words to describe it. In the past year Harry had
been involved in several car accidents. He had sideswiped a bus
in a hit-and-run. He had driven into a light post when drunk.
He had backed his truck down a gully and totaled his mother's
Lexus by driving into the concrete wall of a store when dis-
tracted by a lit marijuana joint that fell into his lap. He'd been
stopped by police for drinking, smoking, speeding, and numerous other infractions, and was due in court the following week.

"What do I mean?" I finally explained. "How many more
times is he going to be so lucky."

"Lucky?" his father said, irritated. "He wrecked three
cars. He's probably going to lose his license. And I'm embar-
rassed to tell you how much I'm paying to fix our cars and
keep them insured for Harry to drive."

"Lawyers, too," Harry's mother added.

"He could have hurt or killed himself—or someone else," I
said seriously. "You think it can't get any worse," I went on
feeling that I was talking to parents who themselves might be
adolescents. "It can."

"What are we supposed to do?" his mother asked.

"Tell him he can't drive your cars?"

They nodded in resignation.

"But he's finally gotten himself a job," his mother said, as
if pleading with her dad to go to the prom. "He needs a car
to deliver newspapers,"

"I don't know," Harry's father said to me. "I hear you.
But I don't think we can do that."

My plea that they protect Harry from himself couldn't change his parents' mind, but fortunately he could. On their way home, they saw him and friends loading Harry's truck with beer. They'd purposely driven home the long way past the abandoned railroad station where Harry and his friends hung out. My confronting Harry's parents hadn't convinced them to deny his right to drive, but it had unsettled them enough to wonder.

I've seen it take a long time for some (loving) parents to see that asking their son, who struggles with his own drug problems, to be their designated driver for their own night of drinking may give the wrong message. I've met scoundrel fathers who truly cannot fathom how it is that their own sons lie and connive. It is tough and painful work for parents to own their own responsibilities, blame, and mean words. I've met many immature parents who pour fuel on their child's dislike for teachers and authority. Through usually slow steps, I encourage parents to see their own hypocrisies, contradictions, and moral lapses. It is nearly always worthwhile, however, as parents' blind spots can block their child's changing for the better as severely as Jersey barriers stop traffic. We want to make these mothers and fathers get it as soon as we can. Unfortunately, dramatic and noisy in-your-face tactics with parents seldom help the child who lives in that situation with those parents day after day. Parents, so my experience has taught me, can look at themselves only under the same conditions that their teenage children can—with therapists who care, listen, support, and respect them.

My confrontations are not always so stark, or so set against the forces of drink and drugs, abuse or neglect. With just as careful a mix of gentle and tough, I ask other parents to see how over-doing their well-intentioned love can excuse their children from the consequences of life, depriving them of natural experiences that promote resilience and self-esteem. I poke parents to ponder how their own anxieties and insecurities resonate with their children's, or how their self-directed criticism taps into their children's self-disregard. *"Why,"* my questions and listening ask parents over time, *"can't you see who your child really is, why can't you see how wonderful, beautiful, lovable she is?"*

HELP PARENTS

I hope I do not insult anyone's intelligence by saying this out loud. Parents need therapists' help. Consider the many ways in which we can be of assistance.

> *"Sometimes when I'm driving home, I just . . ."* Glenna's *mother squeezed one hand in the other. She closed her eyes.*
> *"What?" I asked quietly.*
> *"I'm not saying it."*
> *I waited.*
> *"It's too mean. A mother shouldn't think like this."*

Glenna was not an easy child to parent. She bit, scratched, and kicked her devoted mother. Her special needs required her mother's attention around the clock. Her mother had given up a career and friends, not to mention a lot of sleep in order to care for Glenna. I'd never heard one complaint.

> *"But mothers do," I said. "All the time." Her lips trembled.*
> *"Sometimes, when you're driving home, you just, you just what . . ." I prompted.*
> *"I just want to drive right past the house and keep going."*
> *"Where?"*

"I don't care," she replied, breaking down. "Anywhere, far away. I'm so tired." She rested her head in her hands. "I'm just too tired to do it anymore."

How could she not have been tired and frustrated and had moments when she wished she hadn't been a mother, or at least, hadn't been Glenna's mother? Some parents believe that to act saintly they have to think saintly. Nothing is farther from the truth. Glenna's mother gradually learned how to complain and feel sorry for herself. Her loving mothering did not diminish, but the stress of it did. Therapists can help parents by doing nothing more than giving them a place to protest the frustration they suffer or to mourn the lot that their parenting lives have dealt them.

Sometimes, we educate, as when we help parents to understand a learning problem and its implications for home and school, or when we help them to see and meet the needs of a child with an attention deficit. I've helped parents understand what diabetes will mean for their child, enabling them to help their own daughter comply with the difficult medical challenge she faced. My frequent role as consultant to parents' decisions on schools, teachers, and such, resides mostly in my giving them information. As therapists we have experience and knowledge of development and childhood that we lend to parents to put to good use at home. We encourage as when we bolster a single mother who is working hard to be a tougher disciplinarian with her wayward teenage son. And we can even praise, as when that same woman comes in to tell us with pride how she set a curfew and stuck to it. Mostly we provide whatever support we can that helps parents do better by their teenagers.

EPILOGUE

The hospital referral said that 14-year-old Dustin had tried to hang himself. He'd actually attempted to strangle himself, not that the distinction mattered. He'd tied a belt around his neck and had tightened it as hard and for as long as he was able. Thank goodness, his arms and will to die both tired. He was rushed to the hospital where he was found physically fine but severely emotionally troubled.

In our first hour, I was more than half-expecting Dustin to bolt. He looked more uncomfortable than any child I'd ever sat with. He'd spoken few words, answering my yes-or-no questions with a near inaudible grunt. Turtles and snails seemed carefree extroverts compared to how withdrawn he looked and felt. To think of him as brittle, fragile, and as needing my walking on eggshells was inadequate. He wasn't that robust. He could say nothing about his stay in the hospital, his attempt to kill himself, or what life was like up to that point. He looked to be lost inside a dark shroud.

"Do you want to be here?" I asked at the hour's end, know-
ing the answer, wanting only to give him one good chance to
say something that he meant.
He shook his head no and walked out.

As I watched him leave my office, I wondered to myself.
What ever makes me think I can help that boy? If I'd then been
candid with myself, I'd have been unable to see him coming
out of that lonely and painful place. Imagine what kind of hurt
and discouragement leads a healthy young teenager to kill himself, or to try to. What violence. Murderous rage turned toward
oneself, or at best, an impulsive (or measured and planned) act
to relieve unbearable hurt or yet, worse, numbness. When a
child stops feeling, he loses much of the life energy that coun-
ters those inevitable moments of gloom and hopelessness.

For weeks and months, Dustin sat in his chair, fiddling with a
building block or pipe cleaner. He'd say nothing, looking everywhere but at me. His eyes darted, he panted, his brow furrowed,
his feet tapped, as if readying for flight. He was a cornered ani-
mal wanting to run, but feeling trapped and liable to bite. "You
are free to go to the waiting room," I'd said in one of our first
hours. I'd shown him how the door to the office had no lock, and
how he could go in and out as he chose. Over many weeks, he'd
try it himself, leaving for a minute, then returning, repeating it
several times week after week. Never did I mention it, or ask
how it was, why he'd left, or why he'd returned. Only once, after
he'd gone out in a pouring rain, did I do anything. I offered him
some paper towels to dry off. He took them with neither a thank
you nor a glance, and dropped them unused into the wastebasket. Three months into therapy, he still didn't need my help.

Dustin was back in school. He was flunking most subjects
and disrupted his classes. At home he was forever throwing re-

lentless tirades in which he'd verbally assault his mother and younger brother, sometimes pushing them. His explosions were usually triggered by some invisible frustration or slight that no one else noticed. "He's a Dr. Jekyll and Mr. Hyde," his mother said. She decided that he was either bipolar or schizophrenic on top of his major depression, attention deficit, oppositional disorder, and who knows what else. What I was sure of was that here was a boy who lacked any good feeling about himself. Though I wasn't at school to see or hear for myself, I knew that the casual remarks and slights of daily teen life stuck in him like sharpened thorns made of rusted steel, minute by minute proving his self-worthlessness to himself, and in his egocentric mind, to everyone else, too.

Several months into therapy, Dustin still sat hunched in his chair. He pulled the hood of his sweatshirt forward, a hermit among monks. I no longer asked questions. They went nowhere and just led to his having to escape the office. "It must feel awful to need my help," I said. I hoped that voicing his reluctance might make it easier to be here with me.

"Fuck you," Dustin mumbled on his way out. He spent the rest of his hour pacing in my driveway. I thought of going after him. I didn't.

But he came the next week, showing me some connection. Was it a wish to live, to feel better? Was it a gesture of desperation, his last best chance for survival? Or maybe, he just had no other place to go. I didn't make the same mistake, though. I made new ones.

"Dustin," I began, more than halfway through another one of our momentously inert hours, "I spoke to Ms. Chaquette, your teacher this morning. She—"

This time Dustin didn't even bother to curse me. He just left,
never hearing how I'd lobbied for her to give him some space,
or, in his words as I'd fancied them, "to get the fuck off his fuck-
ing back." I looked through the waiting room window and saw
him pacing the driveway with the agitation of a caged tiger.

It's odd how the adult therapist or parenting mind can work. I
worried about his being alone in my driveway. And yet, where
had he ever encountered real danger? Only at his own suicidal
hands. I've seen parents not allow their teen children to go
swimming, or take a subway, or ride their bicycles to the park
out of fear that they will be hurt—children who had stabbed,
cut, poisoned, and otherwise tried to destroy themselves. But
then, he was there on my time, under my watch, wasn't he?

Over the next few months Dustin showed some movement
toward me. He now came to sessions with his things—model
airplanes, his stamp collection, an erector set. He'd sit at my
desk and work. Though he didn't speak about himself or his
project, he'd occasionally curse over some frustration which,
when I asked, he'd describe. His complaints generally implied
that somebody, somewhere had screwed up and left him to suffer because of it. "The nut is threaded in reverse." "They mis-
printed the stamp." I mostly listened and nodded. "Bummer,"
was about the most he could tolerate. Anything more, even
something that I thought might be empathic to his perspective,
wounded him and made him feel blamed.

"Those fucking idiots gave me two left decals for the tail."
"That must be frustrating," I said.
Dustin took his palms and crushed the plastic plane he'd
built. He threw it in the trash then returned to his seat, arms
crossed, his chest heaving.

"But it was so beauti—"

Dustin held up his hands to silence me. He studied me as I walked to the trash can and removed the plane he'd made then destroyed.

"I don't know exactly what happened," I said. "But I think this plane has something to do with how you feel about yourself.

Dustin pulled his hood over his head. Though I couldn't see his face, I saw him use his sleeve to wipe his eye.

Just as I do with parents, I ever have to remember that progress comes in baby steps. Look for it in small ways, I tell parents— a slightly quicker smile, a never before seen helping hand, a fuse that is a couple of millimeters longer. I commonly hear adolescent patients complain that their parents don't even notice their best efforts to change. *Why should I even bother*, they wonder. *What difference does it make?*

"He comes and tells us that he disobeyed and we're supposed to be happy about that," parents will ask me. "Well, for the past years he's disobeyed and lied about it," I'll reply. "It's a beginning, isn't it?" Kicking your foot through one door a year is one door too many, but it is far better than seven doors and four windows. Change doesn't come overnight; it is slow, hard-fought, and ever prone to backslides.

And so, I deliberately point out those modest gains that are easy to miss in the everyday stress of home life. *Look at this! How about that? Has anything gotten better, even something trivial?* He still lies, but he's confessing afterwards. She still doesn't do her homework, but she's bringing her backpack home. She's still afraid of people, but she did stand outside the gym to see what people wore to the dance. Helping parents to notice and appreciate that gains come inch-by-inch brings them double rewards: they avoid undermining their child's work and they are enabled to see signs of progress that will buoy them and their support of the child and her treatment.

It was time to take my own advice. We'd been meeting for near a year and Dustin had not tried to hurt himself or anyone else, though he forever threatened to. He took his medication (which helped), and he'd rejoined his favorite activities, including his church youth group and skateboarding. School had stabilized. His grades had gone from Fs to Cs and Bs, and he was getting many fewer detentions. Yet, his exquisite susceptibility to feeling slighted, ridiculed, and rejected continued. At home, simply spilling some milk or mistyping a word could lead to his noisily rebuking a dairy bottler or keyboard manufacturer, assaults that always boomeranged into a suffocating avalanche of shame and suicidal threats.

Dustin lived what was probably the truest truth of any that I believe as a therapist. There is no more lethal toxin than self-hatred. The slightest misstep or a meaningless glance from a peer was sufficient to trigger his self-critique, harsher than that of any medieval judge. Living in Dustin's head, under the hateful eye of his unforgiving conscience, was a meaner place than any torture chamber envisioned by Poe. Gradually, while building his models and placing stamps in his catalogs, Dustin talked of his frustrations.

> "I can't do anything right," he said, when he'd been unable to get a plane wheel perfectly straight. "I feel worse about nothing than real devils feel about doing horrible deeds."
>
> "You got that one perfectly right!" I replied. Dustin listened with sadness, neither fleeing nor withdrawing.
>
> "At least I got one thing right."

Dustin's therapy was hardly smooth sailing. A wish to die lingered behind every self-doubt or trip of life. "Being me is like getting along with a neighbor that you can't stand and who hates your guts" was how he put it. I frequently made comments that unexpectedly shamed him, but each time we needed a little less time and effort to patch the relationship and to move on. Dustin increasingly seemed to take responsibility for being so tender. "It's not your fault," he'd say, when I'd acknowledge my insensitivity. "I know I take things the wrong way."

As he grew more robust, Dustin's talents and work ethic rose up. His grades improved and he made honor roll. Peers admired him for his skateboarding and his generosity. He held two jobs and his bosses highly valued and trusted him. "They promised me jobs forever, though they think I'll probably go to college." I was not surprised to hear how he'd become as trustworthy as his employers believed him to be. I'd seen adolescents do it enough times to know it wasn't a fluke. And through it all, in spite of all his achievement, Dustin wondered whether he should stay alive.

And you should know he was making this headway much on his own. Dustin's parents were both successful and busy professionals with big jobs. Work was their priority. I seldom saw them, even during the many crises. It would take several weeks of phone tag to make an appointment with them that would usually be canceled last minute with flowery apologies and thank yous for my work with their son. During meltdowns at school, the principal or counselor would often call me because they couldn't locate either parent, or each had pawned the problem onto the other spouse. I thought of taking a clinically righteous stand: I can't treat your son if you won't do your share to help in the treatment. But I feared that such a stance would have led to their taking Dustin out of therapy, so I settled for our rare meetings and occasional phone calls. As it was, his mother once stuck her head out of her new car to complain about the modest copayment that their insurance hadn't covered. I accepted the reality that Dustin lived with, and I shared it, too. We plodded along by ourselves.

> *"What do you think?"*
>
> *"It's delicious," I said. Dustin had brought two whole plates of food that he'd cooked himself. "You didn't have to bother, though."*
>
> *"It was no bother," he insisted.*

Gratitude. A complicated concept, especially in a teenager. For years Dustin had felt so mistreated by the world that he carried a major chip on his shoulder. To him, thankfulness was a luxury for people who should be thankful, people who got what they wanted; and he knew he wasn't one of them. Dustin's envy was malignant. He resented everyone who got what he didn't, even if it was something he didn't want. His feeling gratitude toward me represented a huge gain and was an indicator that his self-hatred was shrinking. For to feel thanks implies that you have received something loving or caring; and to accept something loving or caring requires that you feel deserving of those gifts.

Dustin and I continue to meet. He only recently has begun to complain about his home, and his parents, and the ways in which he's felt neglected and unloved. Only recently, after many hours, has he begun to use therapy the way we think of, coming in and sitting down to talk about what's on his mind. His self-dislike has steadily faded as his self-respect has grown. He's made nicer friends and has grown more tolerant of teachers being who they are. Most of all, he's come to sometimes accept himself and to have compassion for what it can be like living under an inner regime as tyrannical as his own.

"Do you have any idea how fucked up it is to be me?" Dustin asked in his latest hour. I smiled, thinking about his fine report card, his many accomplishments, and all his astonishing growth. "Oh, you're useless," he went on, tossing me a stick of gum. "I don't know why I even bother to talk you."

A FINAL WORD

Adolescence is a trying time for the teenagers who live it as well as for the adults who try to help get them through it. Few teens fly through unscathed. Many more make it with various forms of angst, difficulty, stress, and misery. As one teen patient suggested when his mother asked how kids cope with adolescence, *"We persevere."* The teenagers that you'll meet in your offices will probably be the ones who have the toughest time with or during adolescence. The fact that you as a clinician have made the effort to read this book suggests that you already appreciate how precariously these adolescents walk from childhood to adulthood. You grasp how it is they can all at once want to be babied and treated like adults; let go but not abandoned; confirmed but not intruded on; full of bravado even with their vulnerability. What's more, you like them, not in spite of the dichotomous impossibilities that tortuously push and pull the teenager, but because of them. In the end, even as I like to think that this book may come to help you in your important work, I recognize that it will be your basic and genuine good feeling, high regard, respect, and concern for who and where these children-to-adults are that will matter most. I realize those will be the critical factors that most engage and settle adolescents into their therapies with you and send them back out into the world and their lives on a surer and more hopeful footing.

INDEX